Social Education
and
Personal Development

Social Education
and
Personal Development

Delwyn and Eva Tattum

David Fulton Publishers
London

David Fulton Publishers Ltd
2 Barbon Close, London WC1N 3JX

First published in Great Britain by
David Fulton Publishers 1992

British Library Cataloguing in Publication Data

A catalogue record for this book is available from the British Library

ISBN 1-85346-110-5

Typeset by Chapterhouse, Formby, L37 3PX
Printed in Great Britain by BPCC Wheatons Ltd. Exeter

Contents

Figures and Tables

Foreword

Japan is quite explicit in its policy of schools developing more than the intellect of their pupils. Both the overt and covert curriculum include a substantial component of social and moral education not just as talk and simulations but as functional experience. Japanese pupils learn to help each other with their studies. They are expected to socialise each other. They are expected to work and play in groups where respect and concern for others is encouraged. Teams of pupils organise and run the domestic side of school life. Individuals learn to flourish in group contexts.

England and Wales subscribe to a similar rhetoric of educating 'the whole person', but in fact emphasise adult control and are more likely to preach about responsibilities than require pupils to exercise them. 'Personal and social education' was introduced more as an additional subject than as a pervasive principle. It is prone to be devalued as light relief from learning lessons.

Delwyn and Eva Tattum open up the whole range of issues and possibilities of social education and personal development. Their opening chapters set the problems in context and are a strong reminder of the social nature of human beings; we are not individual islands to be 'shaped' by threats of punishment and offers of rewards, but the manner and use of such incentives will be crucial for the qualities of the personal beings that emerge from homes and schools.

Part 2 explores the relevance of the school as an organised community and proceeds to examine the role of both teachers and peers as influences on individuals, bringing the opportunities to life with examples and cases.

The authors are clear that schools have to be concerned with developing and establishing certain values in their pupils. There is no escape; it is simply a question of which values and how. Perhaps one of the tragedies of post-war British education is that in our zeal not to be seen as authoritarian and dogmatic, we have become so amorphous that schools (and society) have drifted into aimlessness. If we are to have a sensibly democratic society in which individuals are cooperative members of communities, we need to be efficient in setting up the correct educational contexts to such an end. Delwyn and Eva Tattum offer a wealth of observations and advice on how we might revive a unity of purpose.

Professor Peter Robinson
University of Bristol
January 1992

Preface

We thought long and hard about the title of this book – 'Social Education and Personal Development', as we wished to convey the interactive nature of what we believe happens in classrooms. And whilst the emphasis is on how teachers seek to influence the personal and social development of children this is by no means a one-way process. Teachers too learn about themselves as persons and professionals from the experience of spending 5 hours a day, 5 days a week, with 30 children whose behaviour changes by the minute – individually and as a group. To compare a class at the beginning and end of a school year can be dramatic and salutary. Some changes teachers will have planned and taught to achieve – especially those academic attainments measured within Standard Attainment Targets (SATs). But there will be changes which have not been legislated for and which defy quantification – they will be in the social and emotional development of individual pupils and the class as a whole.

Supplementary questions at this point may be, 'Can teachers really prepare and plan for personal and social development at these different levels?' 'Isn't PSD caught rather than taught?' 'Aren't there many other powerful social influences with which the school has to compete?' We agree that these are relevant questions but also believe most profoundly that they are not good reasons for not having a coherent policy for personal and social education/development in primary schools,

For the last twenty years or so secondary schools have worked to improve their organisation and delivery of personal and social education. During that time teachers in primary schools have continued to do what they believe they do best, that is, cater for the social and personal development of children on a day-to-day basis, using naturally emerging formal and informal situations to emphasise and illustrate the kinds of behaviour, attitudes and values they wish to inculcate. But in the present social and educational climate waiting for an opportunity to arise is not good enough, schools need an approach to PSD which is consistent with their approach to all other areas of the curriculum. A curriculum audit in this area will examine their provision, in both the formal and informal 'social curriculum', to the personal and social growth of their pupils across the years. It is because the social curriculum is so diffuse that schools must declare an unity of purpose and objectives to which all teachers subscribe and support. This aspect of children's development is too important to be left to chance – it must be carefully planned and managed. If PSD is to be successfully promoted we must give serious attention to the following points.

(1) The personal and social development of children should be an integral part of a school's ethos.
(2) It should be reflected in the quality of relationships within the school community itself and between the school and its wider community – most especially children's families.
(3) And thirdly, it should be clearly communicated in the aims and objectives of all teachers and other adults in the school, who together have contributed to the planning, development, implementation and management of a broadly defined social curriculum.

The purpose of this book is to provide a *framework* for teachers and other professionals interested in the social and emotional development of children, against which they can examine their own and the school's PSD philosophy and practice. In addition, the book is written for teachers in training or on advanced education courses which include pastoral care in primary schools. The authors believe that practice must be grounded in theory and the book starts by presenting a theoretical perspective based on the precept that *the development of Self is a Social experience*. In this process of learning about ourselves we firstly look at the family as the most influential socialising agency in a child's life and then progress to look at the socialising influences of school and classroom, the nature and quality of relationships provided by teachers and, most importantly, other children. Finally, we extend the framework principle into how we envisage a school could organise a cross-curricular, school-wide social curriculum.

The writing of this book would not have been possible without the cooperation and support of many persons. First of all, our gratitude and appreciation is extended to all the children we have worked with throughout our teaching careers. They showed remarkable forebearance and rewarded us with numerous insights into their social world. We would also like to thank the students who chose to follow an optional course on social and personal development in the primary school. The course was offered to Year 4 B.Ed. students, immediately after teaching practice – a time when they were looking forward to having responsibility for their own classes of children.

Our appreciation also goes to Mrs Margaret Moses, who typed the book with a professional diligence and expertise which helped reduce our panic at critical times.

We have chosen to use the masculine pronoun when writing about children and the female form for teachers.

Delwyn and Eva Tattum
January 1992

Acknowledgements

Grateful acknowledgement is made for reproducing the following tables and quotations in the book: in Chapter 1 a Figure from *Thinking About . . . Personal and Social Education*, editor P. Lang, publisher Blackwell; an attitude scale by L. Cohen and A. Cohen in the *Durham Research Review*, 24, 1970; a model of child-rearing patterns by E.S. Schaefer in the *Journal of Abnormal and Social Psychology*, 59, 1959; three Tables from *Seven Year Old in the Home Environment* by J. Newson and E. Newson, published by Allen and Unwin – all in Chapter 2; and in Chapter 3 a Table on Attendance Rates from HMI publication *Education Observed 13, Attendance at School*, 1989. Also in Chapter 3 the reproduction of an extract from K. Reid's book *Helping Troubled Pupils in Secondary Schools*, Volume 2, publisher Blackwell.

Every effort has been made to contact the holders of copyright but if any have been inadvertently overlooked the publishers will be pleased to make the necessary acknowledgements at the first opportunity.

PART ONE

Socialisation and the Development of Self

The first three chapters address the fundamental issue of socialisation and the development of every child as a 'centre of consciousness' (Peters, 1966). Which means not only a growing awareness of self but also respect for other persons. In Chapter 1 we present a theoretical approach which is particularly appropriate to a study of socialisation, as its focal concern is the *self is social*; and in the personal and social education of young children the way social experiences occur has a major bearing on personal development. The approach is called Symbolic Interactionism and in subsequent chapters its main concepts will be applied to social education and personal development in primary schools. Chapter 2 is about socialisation in the home, as it is here that a child's basic learning of values, beliefs, attitudes, customs, habits and, most importantly, language, takes place. The quality and nature of that learning has a significant influence on how well a child adjusts to early schooling. Entry into school means adopting the role of pupil and all that entails. In Chapter 3 we focus on pupil socialisation into the ways of the school by examining the progress of pupil career from reception class to year six. For many it is a smooth and satisfying learning experience in which their self-images are sustained and enhanced. Unfortunately, other children have discordant and negative experiences of schooling. Even in infant classes teachers can identify those who they predict will have deviant pupil careers, causing trouble for themselves and problems for teachers.

Within home and school we therefore look at how social experiences and learning are organised and presented to young children so that parents and teachers may better work together for each child's personal development in the social as well as cognitive domains. To that purpose we offer the following poem, which contains the basic

2

principles which influence how each and every child comes to feel about him/herself from the way in which adults and other children respond to them in their day by day encounters.

> If a child lives with criticism
> He learns to condemn
> If a child lives with hostility
> He learns to fight
> If a child lives with ridicule
> He learns to be shy
> If a child lives with shame
> He learns to feel guilty
> If a child lives with tolerance
> He learns to be patient
> If a child lives with encouragement
> He learns confidence
> If a child lives with praise
> He learns to appreciate
> If a child lives with fairness
> He learns justice
> If a child lives with security
> He learns to have faith
> If a child lives with approval
> He learns to like himself
> If a child lives with acceptance and friendship
> He learns to find love in the world
>
> (Source unknown)

CHAPTER 1

Socialisation and Social Interaction

Introduction

The twentieth century has witnessed dramatic changes in the nature of processes of socialisation. In a period of rapid change the challenge has been to prepare people of all ages, not just the young, to be able to cope with the demands made by the complex nature of modern, urban, industrial society. As the main agent of socialisation the family has experienced changing patterns of child-rearing, a decrease in family size, its further dispersion from the extended family, plus the changing position and role of women. These factors affecting the family and community will be elaborated on in the next chapter, as will the increased involvement of other agencies in supplementing the family's socialisation of the young. With the increased growth of services a range of professional views have been promulgated about correct ways of bringing up children. Amongst the groups spreading the message are health visitors, antenatal clinics, family doctors, community nurses and obstetricians, all of whom stress the importance of the early years of life for future development. A growing interest in childhood is also evident from the growth in the number of magazines devoted to bringing up young children and the increase in the number of specialist stores whose goods are exclusively marketed for children. There are toys and games for different age groups, graduated reading books and pre-teen boutiques, added to which is the power of advertising through newspapers, magazines, radio and television, to convince parents of the importance of childhood socialisation.

The introduction of full-time, compulsory education has also contributed to the professionalisation of socialisation, and equally influential has been the extension of the time children spend in school. The most significant expansion has been in the raising of the school leaving age but, in recent years, social and economic pressures have demanded increased provision for the rising fives. These developments have uncompromisingly made schools second only in importance to the family in the early socialisation of children, an aspect of which has been the growing emphasis being placed on personal and social education (PSE) in primary schools. In subsequent chapters a particular theoretical approach to personal and social development will be presented, it goes under the label of Symbolic Interactionism (SI). In this chapter we will present the central concepts of SI and these will be applied in the following chapters as we examine a whole-school approach to PSE. It will involve looking closely at school organisation and classroom management and the nature and quality of social experiences we give children; teacher–pupil interactions and relationships; peer group influences and also, how the whole curriculum may be used as a vehicle for social education and personal development.

What is socialisation?

Socialisation is a critical concept for all the social sciences because in considering it we are forced to examine the relationship between the individual and society. In examining it we are essentially exploring how we each became the kind of person we are. In fact, it would be valuable if you were to reflect on the evidence of your own experiences and also observe children (and adults) in your own family and classes you teach. For what we are seeking to understand is how the newborn infant becomes an adult member of society. But socialisation is more than formal education. It includes the acquisition of values and beliefs, attitudes and habits, skills and language, transmitted through the family, peer groups and mass media, as well as the school. These agents of socialisation are not mutually exclusive neither do they necessarily work in harmony, so that the process experienced by each of us is exceedingly complex, with varying degrees of consensus and conflict in the messages we receive.

It is because socialisation is such a basic concept that we have different theoretical approaches to its understanding. The early theorists in this field were strongly deterministic – whether from a psychological or sociological standpoint. Within the sociological tradition definitions were frequently expressed in terms of the transmission of culture, that is, a straitjacket programme for producing social beings thoroughly integrated into the mould acceptable to society. Theorists in this tradition saw socialisation as a mechanism for social control, in which the parent becomes a control agent operating in the family and the teacher in the school. Many sectors of society today regard the social control function of the teacher's role as being central and, in fact, the relationship between the well-being of the class and the needs of the individual have to be daily balanced by every teacher. Examples of this approach are contained in the following quotations:

> The process by which society moulds its offspring into the pattern prescribed by its culture is termed socialisation.
>
> (Child, 1943)
>
> We may define socialisation as the process by which someone learns the way of a given society or social group so that he may function within it.
>
> (Elkin, 1960)

But this passive and malleable view of the individual was challenged in an influential article by Dennis Wrong (1961). He called it 'The over-socialised conception of man in modern society'.

> Socialisation may mean two quite distinct things; when they are confused an over-socialised view of man is the result. On the one hand socialisation means transmission of the culture, the particular culture of the society an individual enters at birth; on the other hand the term is used to mean the process of becoming human, in acquiring uniquely human attributes from interaction with others. All men are socialised in the latter sense but this does not mean that they have been completely moulded by the particular norms and values of their culture.
>
> (Wrong, 1961)

Wrong was highly critical of the conservative function of social determinism which stresses the preservation of society as paramount; he wished to draw attention to the active part played by the individual in developing personal attributes in interaction with others. Children are not to be seen as carbon copies of their parents but as active beings capable of innovation and change.

Psychological determination is to be seen in the work of learning theorists who also neglect innate factors and see socialisation as the 'shaping' of behaviour in response to externally applied reinforcements. Their *tabula rasa* view of human nature is well illustrated in the following:

> Give me a dozen healthy infants, well-formed and my own specified world to bring them up in and I'll guarantee to take any one at random and train him to become any type of specialist I might select – doctor, lawyer, artist, merchant-chief and, yes, even beggar-man and thief,

regardless of his talents, penchants, tendencies, abilities, vocations, and race of his ancestors.

(Watson, 1924)

Lest it should be thought that such behaviourist views have been abandoned a more recent quotation illustrates how learning theorists see activity as initiated by events from outside the person rather than orginating from within.

The child is born empty of psychological content into a world of coherently organized content. Like a mirror, however, the child comes to reflect his environment; like an empty slate he is written upon by external stimuli; like a wax tablet he stores the impressions left by these stimuli; and like a machine he may be made to react in response to stimulating agents . . . the child's behaviour increasingly reflects the coherence of external reality as he grows up.

(Langer, 1969)

The above tradition was derived from the work of Watson, Pavlov and others, and more recently developed by Skinner. The processes they focused on through which the external world makes its impact on the child are conditioning, imitation and mediation. Behaviourism is based on a mechanistic stimulus–response (S–R) approach in which the acquisition of behaviour is explained in terms of a history of *reinforcement*. The S–R bands are regarded as the basic building-blocks of behaviour and behaviourists declined to make inferences about what goes on within the organism – they are not concerned with hidden process or causes as they are largely beyond direct 'objective' observation. What matters to them is overt behaviour which they assume to be controlled by social forces and which is, therefore, open to manipulation by socialising agents such as parents, teachers and others. Critics of this approach join with Allport (1961) who wrote that 'to leave out this subjective pivot of personality (the sense of self) is to keep the rim but discard the hub of the problem'.

More recently, research and debate about socialisation have increasingly concerned themselves with laying stress on the techniques of the process rather than the end product. There has also been interest in regarding babies as socially responsive from birth and far more actively involved in the interactions they have with other humans. We regard the infant as a being with considerable powers to gather and process information from his surroundings, and although in the early weeks/months his capabilities are limited by adult standards he quickly demonstrates that he is socially aware and responsive. It would seem that from birth the infant is already structured in such a way that he will actively help determine his own experiences.

> ... pre-programmed with some kind of sensitivity towards reciprocal social interaction, the human infant undoubtedly is; but the very nature of this pre-programming implies that within weeks – and perhaps within days or mere hours – after birth he is embarked upon the never-ending programme of social intercommunication with other self-conscious, intelligent, and above all, communicating human beings.
>
> (Newson, 1974)

In the above extract Newson is clearly suggesting that the newly born infant is a far more competent organism than it is given credit for in the theories discussed earlier. Most of what a human infant learns is learned from a dynamic interaction with adult humans – an inanimate environment would provide impoverished stimuli towards an understanding of the world in person to person terms. Recent research into child development has begun to move away from viewing infant behaviour as simply unpatterned and random and begun to look at this two-way, reciprocal interaction rather than concentrating on isolated, one-way messages. Schaffer (1971) reports on what he calls 'social signalling systems', such as smiling, crying and eye contact, which 'show that the infant himself can initiate social interactions and that these signalling devices may be used to regulate the required stimulation obtainable from other people'. It is with the 'growth of sociability' that young babies signal their needs, using a range of pre-verbal and non-verbal social interactions; and it is this view of the infant – child, adolescent and then adult – as active participant in its own socialisation that will be developed throughout subsequent chapters.

The interactionist approach to socialisation

Although the interactionist approach to socialisation is still about fitting individuals and society together, the emphasis is on the person's learning experiences as he adapts to the various situations he encounters each day. This model goes beyond the traditional approach of equating socialisation with the period of maturation and sees the process extending into adulthood – literally from the cradle to the grave. In the following section, socialisation will be discussed under four headlines, namely:

(i)   socialisation is an ongoing, active process;
(ii) socialisation is a reciprocal process;
(iii) socialisation is a life-long process;
(iv) socialisation is a cumulative process.

(i) From the above it is evident that interactionists are interested in understanding the *process* of becoming an active human being rather than seeking to describe the *product* outcome of the socialisation process.

The infant faces a packaged world (Shipman, 1972) in the sense that he has played no part in its production. He can interact with those who interpret it for him but he has no choice in *what* to internalise or in *who* are to be socialising agents. That world is given as absolute and inevitable.

> This packaged world which faces the child is the product of social interaction. Life can only persist if humans can predict the actions of others, and themselves act in ways that are predictable. Habits, customs, rituals and institutions arise during social interaction. But, once established, these patterns of behaviour become ready-made blue-prints for succeeding generations. The child is not just born into a world of adults. He is faced by expectations that have been laid down by many generations before his.
>
> (Shipman, 1972)

Thus the child has to internalise this world in order to interact with those who mediate for him. The learning of language is the most essential element of this process. To learn it is essential to interaction and hence survival, as the child takes on the social world of his socialising agents – mostly parents. But socialisation is not stereo-typing, for, to paraphrase Berger and Luckmann (1967) – man is a product of society, but society is a product of man. The latter point refers to the active involvement of humans as they do not simply accept other people's meanings, but accept, modify or reject them. If people do not just apply previously learned meanings, but revise and modify them through the interpretive process, then they are active participants in the socialisation process. 'Each generation changes the blueprint before handing it on to the next' (Shipman, 1972).

(ii) With age socialisation becomes more of a two-way *reciprocal process*. Much more will be written about reciprocity in interaction in later chapters, but it is sufficient at this point to note that in our lifetime we play many roles, we do not only learn our own role performance but those of our role partners – the people opposite whom we play our roles. For example, a teacher needs to have clear expectations of her pupils', as well as her own, role – this applies to brother–sister, doctor–patient, mother/father–daughter/son relationships. Does not the infant socialise the mother into her role?

The degree of bargaining or negotiating will vary between role partners – often dependent on the power relation that exists. A baby is in no position to bargain with his parents but a teenager is in a much stronger position. Similarly, in primary school, young children have to take what teacher tells them without question but by the sixth form a student may insist on his views being heard.

As an expression of how important reciprocal role learning is, Burns (1986) has written that 'Socialisation is the term applied to the process whereby the individual becomes reasonably predictable to others and other people become predictable to him.'

(iii) Socialisation theorists debate whether what they are examining is a *lifelong process* of continuing adaptation to new roles and situations or a unique and relatively irreversible set of experiences confined to early childhood. For example, Freudians stress the importance of early experiences in the family to adult personality. Suffice it to say that whilst we think there is ample evidence that socialisation does not end with adolescence, it is also the case that early learning is important as it gives an individual a sense of unity within himself and an awareness of his identity. Of particular relevance one would need to consider sex roles, ethnic identity and even social class awareness.

Berger and Luckmann (1967) point out that *primary socialisation* is the *sine qua non* for the successful integration of new members into society. For primary socialisation, which is mainly concerned with childhood, not only means the acquisition of knowledge but also the internalisation of a firm belief that this knowledge is right. In their primary interaction, mostly with their parents, children not only take on the socialising agents' identities but also their social worlds. Primary socialisation is the internalisation of cultural elements that at the time have the character of absolutes.

Doubt, questioning and reinterpretation occur later, when individuals begin to choose between alternative and often contradictory institutions, groups, values and beliefs. Doubt and choice are part of the *secondary socialisation* process which is a life-long process through school, work, marriage, parenthood and, finally, old age.

To design an experiment which would test the centrality of early social learning would be difficult, however situations have occurred 'naturally' which provide a partial answer to the question. In a classic article, Davis (1947) describes the cases of Anna and Isabelle, two children who were 'brought up' under conditions of extreme isolation from others. Isabelle was the illegitimate child of a deaf-mute mother, and she spent most of her first six years alone with her mother in a darkened room. In his description of Isabelle, Davis wrote,

> When she communicated with her mother it was by means of gestures. . . . Her behaviour toward strangers, especially men, was almost that of a wild animal manifesting much fear and hostility. In lieu of speech she made a strong croaking sound. In many ways she acted like an infant.
>
> (Davis, 1947)

Davis suggested that after discovery it appeared that it would be impossible to train Isabelle. That is, she was not capable of benefiting from the lessons she was given – she had not learned the basics and therefore she could not progress. However, once the initial breakthrough was made 'she went through the usual stages of learning characteristic of the years from one to six not only in proper succession but far more rapidly than normal'.

In the case of Anna, who was similarly deprived, progress was slower and at the time of her death at the age of ten she was still far from normal. The reason for her slow advancement is not clear – she may have been congenitally retarded. Though Davis suggests the problem was that she never received the prolonged and expert attention Isabelle received. 'Had Anna . . . been given a mastery of speech at an earlier point *by intensive training* her subsequent development might have been much more rapid' (Davis, 1947).

Though this evidence is by no means unequivocal, these instances do support the motion that though the kind of socialisation we are considering normally occurs at an early age, these cases indicate that early training is not essential. When both girls were found they were about six years of age, and though this made things much more difficult, it was not an insuperable barrier.

(iv) Finally, socialisation is a *cumulative process*, as each individual does not begin afresh in each new situation but builds on previous knowledge, that is, he takes into each new situation a set of previous social learning. Which means that we are not all that free today from what we experienced yesterday!

The last point is very important for teachers to appreciate. Within the family the young child is unlikely to encounter any great discrepancies between past and present experiences – there is continuity. But when he starts school he may find discontinuity as his past experience may not have prepared him for the new social situation.

> The child's ability to learn and even his image of himself may be hampered by the lack of fit between the situations organised by the teacher and those he has experienced in his own family or local community.
>
> (Shipman, 1972)

This aspect of discontinuity between socialising agents and their different expectations will be returned to time and again through the book, most especially in Chapter 5.

Symbolic Interactionism and socialisation

Symbolic Interactionism (SI) is more a constellation of concepts than a tightly integrated body of theory and in this section the intention is to deal with the core of ideas which revolve around the process of socialisation. Then, in subsequent chapters, each of these concepts and others will be applied to the process of personal development as it takes place in the family but, more especially, in the school. A diagrammatical presentation of these concepts can be found in Fig. 1.

It is to George Herbert Mead (1863–1931) that we must turn for the theoretical development and articulation of the main ideas contained in SI, though contemporaries of Mead, such as GH Cooley, John Dewey and WI Thomas, were also active in the development of an interactionist approach to human behaviour. The thoughts of GH Mead were published posthumously, mainly through the energies of one of his foremost disciples, Herbert Blumer, and the transcripts of students who attended his lectures. It was Blumer who, some years later, gave the label Symbolic Interactionism to this school of sociological thought. In this exploration of socialisation the contribution of most of the aforementioned writers will be drawn upon, as well as the developmental and interpretive work of more recent scholars in this field.

Symbolic Interactionism is within the tradition of 'social action' approaches to our studies of the social world and human behaviour. By 'action' we mean conscious behaviour rather than instincts, needs or drives which have more innate origins. In fact, the most basic element running through SI is the dynamic interaction between man and society. This dialectic relationship stresses the importance of viewing the 'self' in human beings as a process and not a structure, active and responsive not passive and fixed. This interdependent relationship runs contrary to the theories discussed so far, for they interpret human behaviour from a predominantly unidirectional, deterministic position. But for SI behaviour is directed by the way a being actively 'interprets' his present situation, and not 'caused' by various internal forces (instincts, needs, drives, etc.) or external forces (social factors such as social class, family background, neighbourhood, etc.). In other words, behaviour is not predetermined and released but is constructed as the individual reflects on the physical situation he occupies, taking into account others who are present, his own review of the situation in the light of previous experiences, and with cognisance of future consequences. It is the process of self-interaction that is active in forming and guiding human conduct. Man does not simply react; he evaluates, criticises and defines, and then acts in the light of his own interpretation and construction of reality.

The self is social

What evolution has produced is a potential for human behaviour but that potential is not realised unless a person engages in social interaction, as studies of feral (wild) children or the cases of isolated children discussed earlier have shown. Therefore, in order to understand how each of us acquires a self is a problem of socialisation – biology is not enough! An essential tenet of SI is that social experience is unique as we each acquire an unique social self through the universe of social experiences in which we engage, and also through the creative reflexivity by which we give meaning to our social environment. Thus socialisation is not viewed as a constraining straight-jacket but as a blueprint to be interpreted.

Our starting point is an understanding of the emergence of self, that is, an understanding of how a tiny, asocial infant eventually becomes a social person. Fundamental human questions are 'Who am I?'; 'What kind of person am I?'; 'Why am I me?'. These questions and attempted answers have no meaning outside social interaction, for in Mead's words 'the self is social', thus emphasising the growing awareness the child has of himself as he experiences interaction with others in an ever widening circle of social contacts. Mead defines self 'as that which can be object to itself, that which is reflexive, i.e. which can be both subject and object'. This means that the human being can be the object of his own actions just as he can act towards other persons. He can analyse and criticise his own behaviour and motives. Similarly, he can modify his actions in the light of self indications as he reviews his action and its effect on himself and others.

> Interactive life is a constant flow of self indications and through 'internal conversation' human action is both purposive and creative. It is creative when an individual faces a new situation, and purposive as the individual takes into account consciously held purposes, plans and knowledge. In other words, through 'reflexivity' human beings are acting and not merely responding organisms.
>
> (Tattum, 1988)

To summarise, the reflexive self incorporates two ideas:

(i) that people have a view of themselves and that they evaluate this self-view, and
(ii) this self-view is based upon and can ultimately only survive within certain sets of relationships.

This means that self is not seen as some immutably fixed entity, but as constantly changing and precarious, though each person develops, over time, an enduring central core which is less immediately vulnerable – both aspects are socially derived. Changes in identity can thus result from changes in a person's position in society – his progress (or lack of it) from one status to another. Our identities (or views of ourselves) are under threat constantly, most especially in person-changing institutions such as schools. An extreme view of this position is that 'teaching is an assault on the self, and resistance to it can be explained as unwillingness to upset one's inner status quo' (Geer, 1968).

In this extract from *Alice in Wonderland* Alice is faced with the question 'Who am I?' because she keeps changing size.

> Alice took up the fan and gloves, and, as the hall was very hot, she kept fanning herself all the time she went on talking: 'Dear, dear! How queer everything is today! And yesterday things went on just as usual. I wonder if I've been changed in the night? Let me think: was I the same when I got up this morning? I almost think I can remember feeling a little different. But if I'm not the same, the next question is, Who in the world am I? Ah that's the great puzzle!' And she began thinking over all the children she knew that were of the same age as herself, to see if she could have been changed for any of them.
>
> 'I'm sure I'm not Ada,' she said, 'for her hair goes in such long ringlets, and mine doesn't go in ringlets at all; and I'm sure I can't be

14

Fig. 1: Personal and social education is interaction

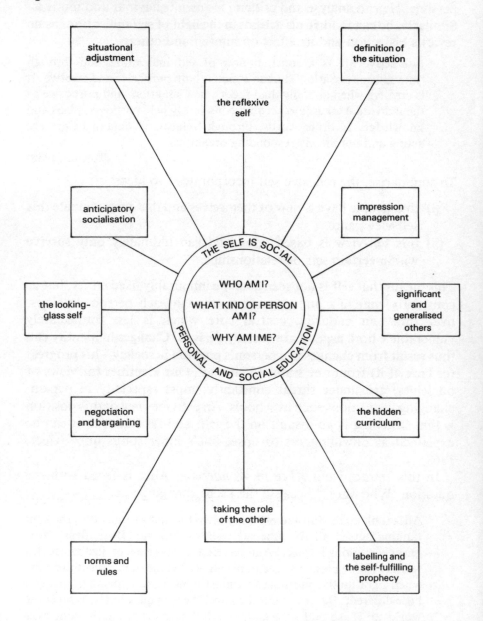

situational adjustment

the reflexive self

definition of the situation

anticipatory socialisation

impression management

THE SELF IS SOCIAL

the looking-glass self

WHO AM I?
WHAT KIND OF PERSON AM I?
WHY AM I ME?

significant and generalised others

PERSONAL AND SOCIAL EDUCATION

negotiation and bargaining

the hidden curriculum

taking the role of the other

norms and rules

labelling and the self-fulfilling prophecy

Mabel, for I know all sorts of things, and she, oh! she knows such a very little! Besides, she's she, and I'm I and – oh dear, how puzzling it all is! I'll try if I know all the things I used to know. Let me see: four times five is twelve, and four times six is thirteen, and four times seven is – oh dear! I shall never get to twenty at that rate! However, the Multiplication Table doesn't signify: let's try Geography. London is the capital of Paris, and Paris is the capital of Rome, and Rome – no, that's all wrong, I'm certain! I must have been changed for Mabel! I'll try and say "How doth the little–" ' and she crossed her hands on her lap as if she were saying lessons, and began to repeat it, but her voice sounded hoarse and strange, and the words did not come the same as they used to do:

> How doth the little crocodile
> Improve his shining tail
> And pour the waters of the Nile
> On every golden scale
>
> How cheerfully he seems to grin
> How neatly spread his claws
> And welcomes little fishes in
> With gently smiling jaws!

'I'm sure those are not the right words,' said poor Alice, and her eyes filled with tears again as she went on. 'I must be Mabel after all, and I shall have to go and live in that poky little house, and have next to no toys to play with, and oh! ever so many lessons to learn! No, I've made up my mind about it; if I'm Mabel, I'll stay down here.

(Lewis Carroll)

In considering further the concept of self it is useful to develop the idea of how we become objects to ourselves. Just as each of us holds opinions about other people so we have opinions about ourselves. Just as we have beliefs about physical objects we hold beliefs about ourselves. This set of beliefs about oneself is called the self-concept, 'the self-concept is the totality of the individual's thoughts and feelings with reference to himself as an object' (Rosenberg, 1979). But there is a distinction between the self-concept and the self, and this should be kept clearly in mind. In Meadian terms the latter is quite clearly not a *structure* but is the *process* of interacting with oneself. We can talk to ourselves, we develop attitudes toward ourselves, predict what we are likely to do and so on. On the other hand, there is a mental structure that can be called the self-concept – the organised set of self-attitudes, which is brought into play in the process of self-communication.

As self-concept is so important in pupil development we would do well to consider it a little further. In a discussion of self-concept Heiss (1981) suggests that it consists of four 'content areas':

(i) *an identity set* – which consists of positional labels which refer to the social categories to which we feel we belong, for example, teacher, student, daughter, parent etc.

(ii) *a set of qualities* – tall, fair, thoughtful, untidy and so on.

(iii) *a set of self-evaluations* – most easily recognised are those attached to identities and qualities in the self-conception, for example, a hardworking student, a good parent, a skilful sportsperson.

(iv) *levels of self-confidence* – this is an important introduction into the self-concept, as it has to do with a person's estimate of the extent to which he or she can master challenges and overcome obstacles.

It is because humans can report on the content of their thought, unlike other animals, that we can investigate people's self-views. The 'Twenty-Statements' or 'Who Am I?' test instructs the subject to 'Ask yourself the question, Who Am I?' and to answer it as if giving the answers to yourself, not to be anyone else. The resulting list of responses is generally taken to be a representation of the person's self-concept. The fact that most people can accomplish the task without difficulty suggests the reality of the self-concept. Limited data also shows that the lists have a fair degree of test-retest reliability. (The self-concept and the Twenty Statement Test are discussed in greater detail later, see p. 102.)

Following that brief digression into self-concept we return to our main concern with the emergence of self. As already indicated the genesis and development of self is found in social relationships, 'it is not initially there at birth but arises in the process of social experience and activity' (Mead, 1956). In his exploration of self Mead concentrated on the process of social interaction by which the individual's consciousness of self emerges, which to Mead is indicative of the existence of 'Mind', that is, the capacity to respond to one's self as others respond to it. The means of acquiring self conception are those of communication in social interaction, for example, through a pupil's relationship with parents, teachers and other children. Much of this learning takes place in the family setting where parents are usually the most *significant others* with whom the child interacts. The child quickly learns that by influencing the feelings of his parents he is able to control in some part what happens to himself. This self-learning process Cooley (1902) named the *looking-glass self*, a concept which describes the self as our imagination of our appearance to others, their judgement of us, and our consequent feelings.

> There are few things more relevant to a child than how people react to him, it is not surprising that the reflections of himself in the eyes of significant others plays a crucial part in the self-concepts a child acquires. From observing the reactions and responses of others to our presentation of self we learn to become the kinds of persons we are – kind, thoughtful, poor at sums, a good reader, and so on.
>
> (Tattum, 1988)

In his exploration of self Mead also concentrated on the process of socialisation as the means by which an individual takes to himself the culture of the social group or sub-groups to which he belongs. Hence the importance of communication, not merely as a facility for receiving and giving off messages, but also for interpreting the infinite number of symbols which humans employ to give meaning to the social environment in which they engage one with another. The meanings that objects, situations and ideas hold for groups have to be learned through primary socialisation in childhood and secondary socialisation throughout adult life.

> It is because we share meanings and hold common understandings that we are able to interpret and predict how others will behave by considering how we would act given the same circumstances. Thus, through engaging in social life a person develops a self; and at the same time acquires the meanings, symbols, and language which make cooperative life possible. Just as SI avoids the accusation of psychological determinism, so the 'over-socialized' deterministic view is avoided as man acquires an unique social self through the universe of social experiences in which he engages, and also through the creative reflexivity by which he gives meaning to his social environment.
>
> (Tattum, 1982)

Mind and symbolic communication

Much of what has been written to this point has taken language for granted. But language makes possible the richness and variety of human social life, and enables each generation to pass on to the next its way of living, skills and knowledge. Animals do not have language in the strict sense of the word, although they have other ways of communicating. Animals can only communicate about things in the present but man's language permits him to talk abstractly about people, places and things in the past and also in the future. Words do not just express thoughts, they help to create them. Most of our thinking is done with words, whether they are spoken or not. The availability of language enormously expands the range of things that can be taught and learned. Without language there would be no thinking. Thinking may not be simply internalised conversation, but it does involve such a process. If we cannot use language, we cannot have a conversation with ourselves, and therefore we cannot think. Mead summarises the constructive association between language and Mind thus, 'Mind arises through communication . . . not communication through Mind.' We are not born with Minds but gain them through interaction with others. This is his riposte to behaviourism, which maintains that only physical behaviour can be observed, thus denying feelings and thought. Between the stimulus and response Mead puts Mind by which we give meaning to our experiences and interpret our own actions.

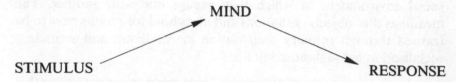

Persons who are deaf, or deaf and blind, require special training if they are to learn a language. Consider the case of Helen Keller's personal description of her discovery of language at the age of seven – she was blind and deaf.

> The most important day I remember in all my life is the one on which my teacher, Anne Mansfield Sullivan, came to me. I am filled with wonder when I consider the immeasurable contrast between the two lives which it connects. It was third of March, 1887, three months before I was seven years old.
>
> The morning after my teacher came she led me into her room and gave me a doll. The little blind children at the Perkins Institution had sent it and Laura Bridgman had dressed it; but I did not know this until afterward. When I had played with it a little while Miss Sullivan slowly spelled into my hand the word 'd-o-l-l.' I was at once interested in this finger play and tried to imitate it. When I finally succeeded in making the letters correctly I was flushed with childish pleasure and pride. Running downstairs to my mother I held up my hand and made the letters for doll. I did not know that I was spelling a word or even that

words existed; I was simply making my fingers go in monkey-like imitation. In the days that followed I learned to spell in this uncomprehending way a great many words, among them pin, hat, cup, and a few verbs like sit, stand, and walk. But my teacher had been with me several weeks before I understood that everything has a name.

One day, while I was playing with my new doll, Miss Sullivan put my big rag doll into my lap also, spelled 'd-o-l-l' and tried to make me understand that 'd-o-l-l' applied to both. Earlier in the day we had a tussle over the word 'm-u-g' and 'w-a-t-e-r'. Miss Sullivan had tried to impress it upon me that 'm-u-g' is mug and that 'w-a-t-e-r' is water, but I persisted in confounding the two. In despair she had dropped the subject for the time, only to renew it at the first opportunity. I became impatient with her repeated attempts and, seizing the new doll, I dashed it upon the floor. I was keenly delighted when I felt the fragments of the broken doll at my feet. Neither sorrow nor regret followed my passionate outburst. I had not loved the doll. In the still, dark world in which I lived there was no strong sentiment or tenderness. I felt my teacher sweep the fragments to one side of the hearth, and I had a sense of satisfaction that the cause of my discomfort was removed. She brought me my hat, and I knew I was going out into the warm sunshine. This thought, if a wordless sensation may be called a thought, made me hop and skip with pleasure.

We walked down the path to the well-house, attracted by the fragrance of the honeysuckle with which it was covered. Some one was drawing water and my teacher placed my hand under the spout. As the cool stream gushed over one hand she spelled into the other word water, first slowly, then rapidly. I stood still, my whole attention fixed upon the motions of her fingers. Suddenly I felt a misty consciousness as of something forgotten – a thrill of returning thought; and somehow the mystery of language was revealed to me. I knew then that 'w-a-t-e-r' meant the wonderful cool something that was flowing over my hand. That living world awakened my soul, gave it light, hope, joy, set it free! There were barriers still, it is true, but barriers that could in time be swept away.

I left the well-house eager to learn. Everything had a name, and each name gave birth to a new thought. As we returned to the house every object I touched seemed to quiver with life. That was because I saw everything with a strange, new sight that had come to me. On entering the door I remembered the doll I had broken. I felt my way to the hearth and picked up the pieces. I tried vainly to put them together. Then my eyes filled with tears; for I realized what I had done, and for the first time I felt repentance and sorrow.

I learned a great many new words that day. I do not remember what they all were; but I do know that mother, father, sister, teacher, were among them – words that were to make the world blossom for me, 'like Aaron's rod, with flowers.' It would have been difficult to find a happier child than I was as I lay in my crib at the close of that eventful day and lived over the joys it had brought me, and for the first time longed for a new day to come.

Not only did Miss Keller's acquisition of words give her an intellectual grasp of the world, but it also altered her attitudes towards things and people and toward herself – there were emotional and conceptual changes to her life.

The transformation was, in short, not merely a superficial one attendant upon the acquisition of an additional motor skill; it was a fundamental and pervasive change that altered, and indeed revolutionized, her total personality and image of herself.

(Lindesmith *et al.*, 1977)

From the above illustration it will be abundantly evident why symbolic communication is central to Symbolic Interaction's approach to an infant's progress towards self-consciousness. Lower animals communicate with each other by what Mead (1956) called a 'conversation of gestures' – a gesture is a social act which stimulates a direct, automatic and non-reflective response from the other animal. A dog will bare its teeth and growl, or a cat will arch its back and spit – and the response of the other animal will be defensive. But, importantly, the first animal does not make its gestures with the express purpose of eliciting certain conceptualized responses, in other words the interaction is devoid of conscious, deliberate meaning and interpretation by either animal of the other's actions. Man's unique ability, on the other hand, is that humans respond to one another on the basis of the intentions or meanings of gestures – the gesture becomes a symbol to be interpreted. For example, the difference can be seen between a punch and the shaking of the fist at someone, for, in the imaginations of the interactants, the gesture symbolically stands for the entire act. Human society is based on shared meanings and common understandings, whereby each individual is able to respond to his own symbolic gestures, thus holding to the same interpretation as do other persons. The most important category of symbols is language; the sound conveys the image. But linguistic communication is more than just an agreed categorisation of an object, important as that is, but it contains within it the idea that the speaker can put himself in the position of the other person and view the situation from his perspective. For example, if a teacher tells a class to 'Sit up straight' or 'Repeat after me', then both pupils and teacher must respond in their minds in the same way. In SI this is called *taking the role of the other*.

Clearly, a person's verbal development cannot take place outside a social group, and reflects the specific group and culture – consider Bernstein's restricted and elaborated codes. Language in large part structures thought and language (Vygotsky, 1962) – although that is not to claim that they are identical. The ability to think abstractly does fully depend on language, and by determining how and what a person thinks, language also greatly determines what a person becomes. It is 'partly responsible for a person's self-concept, identity, personality, attitudes, social and emotional adjustment, in sum his *self*' (Kando, 1977). In the previous paragraph we said that the idea that the speaker can put himself in the position of the other person and view the situation from his perspective is role-taking, that is, the speaker not only reflexively interprets the meaning of his words in his own mind but seeks to actively imagine their interpretation by others. As teachers we must be able to put ourselves in the child's shoes to appreciate learning and behaviour problems. For children it means developing a capacity to take account of the needs of others as well as their own feelings. We each have a repertoire of perspectives which enable us to take on different roles, and with each role-taking we project ourselves into the situation and imagine how we would feel – the better we are able to do this the more we are capable of seeing the other person's point of view. Equally important, it also means we begin to see ourselves as others see us – we become object to ourselves. This action is difficult for young children, and in many teacher–pupil interactions. For some pupils it is a problem of adopting the pupil role, and as the role is not part of his self-awareness he is unable (or unwilling in the case of older pupils) to acknowledge the role of the teacher with whom it is reciprocally linked. For in the process of learning our own role we must learn the role of other or others opposite whom we role play – in learning the role of daughter or son a child must also learn what it means to be mother or father. In the process of learning the role of teacher children play at school.

Thus the process of role-taking is inextricably linked with the concepts of *significant other(s)* and the *generalised other*. Significant others will stand in some position of influence or authority over the child, who comes to regard these people as influential in the organisation of his own behaviour. Infants are born into an inter-connecting network of other individuals – members of the family, friends, teachers, colleagues and acquaintances – all with varying degrees of importance and intimacy. These are members of the infant's social world who provide him with ways of perceiving and defining the world. The infant takes over their standards and attitudes, values and beliefs – and symbolic communications. This is regarded as primary socialisation.

In an extension of the above concept Mead coined the term *generalised other*, to refer to the roles of several others within a whole pattern of group activity. As we interact with several others simultaneously, an individual must place himself in the place of these several others to understand what they collectively are thinking and likely to do. In some cases the generalised other includes people who are not physically present in the interaction situation.

Mead's well-known illustration of taking the role of the generalised other involves the activities of a baseball player, but we may equally consider a football player. For example, before a goalkeeper kicks the ball up field he must take into account the roles of the other members of his team, the opposition players, even referee, linesman and supporters. He must know what they expect him to do before he actually kicks the ball. This is but an illustration and the ability to take the role of the generalised other does not come about through participation in organised games. That ability is there before individuals have any experience of group activities. On the other hand, organised games at school do give children social awareness which takes in the perceptions and attitudes of a wider field of interactants. And teaching, if it is done well, involves a great deal of generalised other role-taking as the teacher asks herself, 'Do the class understand what I am talking about?'

Recent theorists have pointed to more specific 'groups of others' as important sources of self and mental referents, these are *reference groups*. Shibutani (1955) defines the term as 'that group whose outlook is used by the actor as the frame of reference in the organisation of his perceptual field'. Reference groups may be used in a positive or negative way; another distinction is made between comparative and normative reference groups. The former pertains to the groups with which an individual compares himself whilst the latter are those which were (are) the sources of the individual's values. For example, for a disruptive pupil the 'ideal pupil' model professed by teachers and exemplified by 'A' streamers can provide a negative reference group for comparative purposes, whilst his immediate friends will offer a normative reference group whose behaviour he will model in order to achieve and maintain affiliation.

We each identify with different significant others and reference groups, and they, in turn, will provide us with perspectives – or our 'ordered view of life'. Together they are sources of values, beliefs, attitudes and norms – for they are learned and act as constraints or inducements. As part of socialisation, it is a social process whereby the community exercises social control over the conduct of its individual members. As the child takes to himself the culture of the group he progresses from, 'Mother said it's wrong' to 'I know it's wrong.'

Finally, the dialectic relationships between society and the individual is encapsulated by Mead in the dual and reflexive nature of the self as expressed in the concepts of the 'I' and the 'ME'. He writes that 'the self is essentially a social process going on with these two distinguishable phases', and in doing so is referring to two parts of self-interaction rather than two parts of the personality.

> The I is the response of the organism to the attitudes of others; the ME is the organised set of attitudes which one himself assumes. The attitudes of the others constitute the organised ME, and the one reacts towards that as an I.
>
> (Mead, 1956)

'ME' is the conventional, habitual individual, composed of an organised set of attitudes which the individual has learned as a group member. It stands for the roles which have over time been internalised by the individual – without the ME the individual could not be a member of the social group(s). 'I' is the initial, spontaneous aspect of human experience, it is the self acting in the present.

Hence, the ME is the socialised aspect which directs and regulates behaviour along socially prescribed lines, whilst the I is creative and innovative – both are essential to the full expression of self, for in their dialectic interplay they mutually determine one another, as neither represents the total self.

> What Mead wished to express, throughout his work, was the self's two-dimensionality: I am partially the product of the roles I have learned, I am partially socialised, I am partially predictable, and I am partially aware of myself. This is ME. However, I am also more than that, for in the present, I always examine, evaluate and interpret my environment, including my own past behaviour, and how I behave at this time is never a mere reflection of my environment plus my past experience, but always something more. The I, then, indicates the emergent nature of the self and Mead's voluntaristic and humanistic conception of man.
>
> (Kando, 1977)

The ongoing, reciprocal and cumulative process of socialisation is contained in Berger and Berger's (1976) statement 'the biography of the individual, from the moment of birth, is the story of his relation with others.' We speak about our genetic uniqueness (other than identical twins) but SI is about our social uniqueness (including identical twins), as the sum total of each individual's social experiences and subsequent interpretations is different from anyone else's.

Exercises

(1) Consider Alice's predicament. At least our changes of status or identity are not as dramatic as her's but discuss the kinds of problems faced by immigrants or people who suffer from serious accidents which result in facial disfigurement or loss of limb.

(2) Controversy developed over the question of whether Helen Keller could intelligently use words associated with sight and sound. As she was both deaf and dumb, how could she talk of colours and sounds?

(3) In the light of the 'action' perspective developed in this chapter consider the significance of the following poem:

The Humanist's Sonnet

I am determined by my class
I am determined by my sex
I am determined by my God
I am determined by my genes
I am determined by my unconscious
I am determined by my childhood
I am determined by my death
I am determined by my climate
I am determined by my homeland
I am determined by my work
I am determined by my newspaper
I am determined by my deep linguistic structures
I am determined by my etcetera
I am determined to be free

(Anthony Rudolf)

Additional readings

Further application of Symbolic Interactionism to the process of schooling can
  be found in:

Tattum, D. P. (1982) *Disruptive Pupils in Schools and Units*, Chapters 3 and 4.
Woods, P. (1983) *Sociology and the School. An Interactionist Viewpoint*,
  Chapter 1.

CHAPTER 2

Socialisation in the Family

Socialisation or education?

Although the main purpose of this book is to look at social education and personal development in the primary school, it is important for a number of reasons that we consider socialisation in that pre-school period – particularly in the family. Our main reason for adopting this stance is to encourage a broader view of education, which recognises that a great many experiences outside schools are educationally significant. This approach also enables us to study the more formalised and ritualised educational experiences which are exemplified by classrooms, timetables, curricula and examinations, in comparison with the more informal learning processes that shape social behaviour, values and skills.

To emphasise a broader view of education fits in with the life-long process of socialisation developed in the previous chapter. To focus solely on social learning in an educational institution means that we concentrate on the period between the ages of five and sixteen, which is the range of compulsory education for the majority of the population. But this largely ignores the valuable learning and teaching that takes place before compulsory schooling, as well as the contribution made to the educative process by other agencies and institutions, such as the workplace, social clubs, churches, the mass media and so on. Although a study of the above socialising agencies is beyond the scope of this book it is important that we recognise that the family provides an integrating link between agencies and is important educationally to the individual throughout life. In fact, experiences within the family have a profound and continuous influence on personal development throughout life.

In this early discussion of the educational role of the family we are also acknowledging the way in which much of human experience is

27

compartmentalised and identified with particular institutions. Yet, in former times and in other less advanced societies than our own, the family's role in the areas of work, health and education was predominant. We can too easily forget that compulsory education is relatively recent, whereas the process of teaching and learning is one of the timeless features of human society, a feature which distinguishes it from other species.

> In fact, school teaching can be seen as the application, in a highly specialised, concentrated and self-conscious manner, of communication skills which to a greater or lesser degree we all possess, especially in our relationships with young children.
>
> (Open University, E200, 1981)

In addition to the above reasons, the strongest argument for starting with a chapter on teaching and learning in the family is that without due recognition of the educational significance of the family's role our understanding of the education system itself would be incomplete. This interrelationship and interdependency in the realm of social and personal development will be elaborated upon in subsequent pages.

> Educational institutions do not operate in a vacuum, although they often appear to do so through their predominantly child-centred rather than family-centred orientation. Talking about children making 'the transition from home to school' or 'the transition from school to work', disguises the experience of the individuals concerned, which is not of proceeding from one context to the next in a strictly sequenced life-career. We do not cease to be members of families when we first go to school, nor when we first go to work. For the vast majority of us, the family provides a continuous, although changing, background of experiences, against which the influence of generally much more discreet episodes of formal education needs to be set. Indeed, it is the interrelationships between family and schooling that provide some of the central themes of educational study, e.g. the relative influence of family and schooling on attainment; the relationships between parents and teachers; the desirability of extending the school curriculum into topics normally 'taught' with the family (e.g. sex, religion), and the case for pre-school education.
>
> (Open University, E200, 1981)

Before we move on to examine the role of the family in more detail we shall spend some time looking at the degree of agreement that exists between parents and teachers in the area of personal and social education. We will also examine further the relationship between education and socialisation. One of the problems in presenting the following research findings is that they were carried out pre-National Curriculum, which has made the teachers function much more highly specific. The proscriptive nature of the curriculum in core and foundation subjects, plus the emphasis on targets of achievement, may well adversely influence teachers' perception of their teaching functions.

The first example of research into the respective views of teachers and parents tried to identify attitudes towards desirable qualities of the primary school child (Cohen and Cohen, 1970). They asked a large group of primary school teachers and parents of children in their schools to complete a short questionnaire consisting of a series of fifteen scales representing contrasting adjectives on a seven point scale. (This attitude measurement is known as a semantic differential scale in which respondents are asked to mark one interval for each scale, according to whether their views tended towards one or other extreme or were neutral.)

To be successful at school a child should be:

questioning	- - - - - - -	accepting
submissive	- - - - - - -	dominant
hardworking	- - - - - - -	lazy
dull	- - - - - - -	bright
reliable	- - - - - - -	unreliable
disobedient	- - - - - - -	obedient
conforming	- - - - - - -	independent
fast	- - - - - - -	slow
uncooperative	- - - - - -	cooperative
popular		lonely
friendly	- - - - - - -	reserved
considerate	- - - - - - -	selfish
shy	- - - - - - -	confident
impolite	- - - - - - -	polite
dishonest	- - - - - - -	truthful

(Cohen and Cohen, 1970)

Cohen and Cohen found a high level of agreement among parents about the desirability of children being *polite, cooperative and reliable*. Teachers displayed a similar high degree of consensus in their emphasis on children being *cooperative, hardworking and truthful*. And so, whilst both groups emphasised cooperation parents tended to regard qualities of *sociability* as being most desirable, whereas teachers had the greatest concern for qualities to do with the *moral character* of children. When comparisons were made between the groups the pattern of differences varied between infant and junior parents and teachers. There was a much higher level of agreement between infant school teachers and parents than between junior school teachers and parents.

> Junior teachers more than junior parents attached importance to those attributes of the pupils' classroom behaviour which lead to success in a learning climate more child-centred than teacher-centred (independence, questioning, non-accepting, less-conforming). Parents, on the other hand, placed greater emphasis upon qualities such as submissiveness, conformity, and acceptance, findings which substantiate other reports of working-class parental concern for the inculcation of passive roles in their children.
>
> (Cohen and Cohen, 1970)

The second piece of relevant research was conducted by a team based at Birmingham University (Ashton *et al.*, 1974) which surveyed the aims of primary teachers. Three major aims were detected, namely:

(1) the teaching of basic skills – reading, writing and arithmetic;
(2) personal development – positive orientation towards school life, a sense of competence, the development of individuality;
(3) the development of personal awareness and moral understanding.

In effect, teachers in primary schools perceived their functions much more broadly than the central demands of the National Curriculum and expressed their aims as encompassing the inculcation of desirable social and moral qualities. Thus the gap that is frequently presented as existing between teachers and parents may not be too pronounced. If this is the case, and we have no substantive reason to disbelieve it, then teachers would do well to draw upon the support and cooperation of parents in every aspect of the education process. This approach is strongly advocated by the Newsons following their interviews of mothers of seven year olds in their Nottingham study. With particular reference to the teaching of reading they found that whilst schools might wish parents to support the work of the teachers, there seemed little evidence that schools were willing to support parents' efforts by introducing them to some of the techniques and schemes used in teaching reading. From the following quotation it is evident that the Newsons do not believe that a strict role demarcation is in the best interests of childrens' education.

The help parents give may now be ill-informed or ill-directed; it may be too tentative to be effective, out of fear of what 'the school' may say; it may be too little, or too fragmented. But if eighty-one in every hundred parents are trying to help their children with reading and most of them don't know how to, schools are surely not only failing dismally in their educative role, but wasting the most valuable resource they have. A revolution in literacy could be sparked off and fuelled by parents and teachers in determined cooperation.

(Newson *et al.*, 1977)

It may well be that the Newsons' indignation challenges not only *your* personal perception of your role as a teacher but also *your* view of the nature of children's learning. But with an important teaching programme that is in danger of compartmentalising children's education into cognitive, physical, aesthetic etc., where is the place of social and personal education?

The family

From the evidence it would appear that the family in some form has been up to the present day a universal institution and that there is no known society in which it does not comprise a component part of the social structure. But not only is the family universal in time and space, it has also displayed remarkable durability in the face of wars and revolutions, periods of crisis and, finally, experiments with alternatives.

One of the reasons often put forward for alternatives is that the position of women in the family is unsatisfactory. It is argued that men and women should have equal opportunities in life and that it is unjust for mothers to be 'tied to the home' if they want to follow other occupations. This may sound a very modern idea but in the fourth century BC Plato argued that 'abilities are similarly distributed in each sex, and it is natural for women to share all occupations with men.' He wrote in the *Republic* that men and women 'should be forbidden by law to live together in separate households . . . wives should be held in common by all . . . and no parent should know his child, or child his parent'.

In recent history the USSR made attempts from 1917 onwards to undermine the family, for according to Marxist doctrine, stable, monogamous family life is a bulwark of capitalism. Marriage, therefore, in the early days of communism was registered without ceremony, or was valid merely by virtue of a simple declaration of cohabitation; divorce required only an application by one spouse and abortion was on request. At school, children were indoctrinated to put state before family. But the consequences were alarming. It was found that anti-family policies weakened community ties, were associated with violence and hooliganism among the young, and the birthrate fell dramatically, which presented a threat to both the labour force and military recruitment. Consequently, in the thirties the family was reinstated as the training ground for socialist children.

Since the Second World War, a more sophisticated attempt to do without the family has taken place on Kibbutzim in Israel. Here children are reared communally in nurseries staffed by experts, and their parents are relieved of daily responsibility for them. The relationship with parents, though restricted, does exist and they are able to give their children a certain amount of love and security. Some observers claim that in recent years parents have begun to play a great part in child care and socialisation. In certain Kibbutzim parents take evening meals with their children, nurse them when they are unwell, and take a close interest in their choice of friends, their progress in school and vocational aspirations. It is also noted that members of the second generation of parents, with fewer economic pressures and less fired with pioneering zeal, tend to marry out of the Kibbutzim and live in families as do most other Europeans.

The social functions of the family

In the previous section there was clear evidence that societies in general regard the family (regardless of form) to be essential to their continuity and stability. In sociological terms the family fulfils functions which are important to society or which no other social institutions can adequately perform. In reductionist terms the two basic functions are procreation and socialisation, that is, families provide for the renewal and maintenance of society by the creation of new members and their inculcation into society's ways.

In this section we shall briefly examine the wider functions of the family, consider the changes that are taking place and their implications for relationships, and then discuss the perennial question of whether the family is in decline.

All societies find it convenient to make the family responsible for at least the following basic functions.

(1) *The regulation of sexual behaviour and reproduction*
Sexual desires are very powerful and if uncontrolled can lead to jealousies and rivalries which could disrupt the stability of social groups. Therefore, all societies attempt to keep sexual urges within socially acceptable bounds. Rules about mating are obviously related to the birth of children, so through its control of sexual relationships the family is also responsible for reproduction of the young. In this sense birth within the family is socially legitimised, although social attitudes are changing towards birth outside the traditional family structure.

Birth within the family also has to do with social placement and personal identity. It gives the newly born a family name and has to do with legal issues concerning inheritance and succession. Ties of blood and marriage gives one a position in a kinship network.

In Chapter 1 we discussed the concept the self is social, and asked the question 'Who am I?'. In attempting to answer that question we invariably draw upon our family position, for it is this which gives us our early sense of identity and also our status in society – it has to do with a sense of 'worth' in our own eyes and the eyes of others. Where social status is given by circumstances outside one's control, as is the case with family, we call it an *ascribed status*. Progression from being judged according to family background to one's worth as regarded on personal merit is referred to as *achieved status* – on entry into school how well we achieve gains increased importance.

(2) *The satisfaction of other basic needs*
For several years young children are incapable of looking after themselves, so it is essential that adults cater for their protection and general welfare. But the family is not just concerned with the care of children, it also provides for older members who fall ill or become infirm. With many more people living longer, family care for the old is a growing social problem.

The provision of care for all members includes economic consideration such as food, clothing and shelter, and also emotional support by providing a secure and stable base – a refuge in times of stress.

In recent decades the welfare state has partly replaced the support given by kin. In providing social security and welfare services for all the state helps families in times of hardship, but to do this it is often necessary for it to interfere in family life. Implicit in the welfare state is the principle that the whole society takes responsibility for its children, old people, sick and others in need.

(3) *Child-rearing and socialisation*
It is not enough just to produce offspring and care for their basic needs. New members have to be taught what is expected of them and how to relate to other people. They must learn the moral values and beliefs of their culture. They must also learn the language of their group as a basic requisite for survival.

This period which concentrates particularly on pre-school children is called *primary socialisation*. It is at this stage of human development that the interface between the individual and society are most acutely observed. The power imbalance between the carer and infant facilitates the inculcation of socially desirable knowledge and behaviour. It takes place in a *primary group* which is close, intense and continuous in its contact. It is a world with which the infant has nothing to compare. This presentation of socialisation can be interpreted as akin to social control. For socialisation transmits, through gentle and on-going manipulation of sanctions, a pattern of normative values, attitudes and behaviour which are essential for the preservation of good order. But although socialisation and social control are related, they are far from being identical concepts. For socialisation is not indoctrination except maybe at the very earliest stages when the infant has no choice but to respond in certain social ways. But, as developed in the previous chapter, even the very young child is not wholly passive in the mother–child interaction, neither is that interaction just in one direction.

The interactional quality of parent–child relationships has been studied by Schaffer using video-techniques in order to make a very detailed analysis of mother–child interactions during the early years. In a recent essay (Schaffer, 1988) he concentrates on the first year of development – mutual-gazing and vocalisation. He illustrates the quite distinctive strategies that mothers (or other carers) adopt in relationship with their infants. There is a strong orientation to the infant's face, there are exaggerated facial expressions and voice intonations, periods of intense watchfulness, fluctuating tempo of behaviour, shorter length and simplified grammatical structure of utterances and frequent repetitions. Most importantly, these are two-way interactions and not static sets of teaching strategies. Schaffer explains how the rapidly growing child constantly places new demands on the adult's repertoire of skills. In this participatory to-and-fro the young infant learns not merely to respond but to initiate; to regulate the interchange to its own advantage; and at the same time learns to adapt to the specific interactive styles of different partners. The dyadic interchange is a highly intricate process in which the growing child becomes more actively engaged in controlling its own immediate environment.

> ... interchanges gradually become less responsive and more autonomous, that memory of previous encounters begins to exert its influence, and that infants generally become more competent in handling the information presented by the other person with speed and efficiency.
>
> (Schaffer, 1988)

This model of socialisation which stresses interaction also posits an essentially democratic and liberal ethos to role relationships and child-rearing, a theme neatly developed in the following extract.

> The most usual view of socialization is of a learner being exposed to the expectations of others and responding to them. Rewards and punishments are used to inhibit behaviour not approved by the socializer and to encourage those which are approved. But socialization not only occurs through interaction between individuals. The activity of the learner consists not only in interpretation but in intervention. As the learner responds to clues presented by others, he presents them with clues. They learn with him.
>
> This two-way learning process has many important implications. First it means that learning situations can range from those in which there is no room for the learner to influence the teacher, to those where there is give and take. Parents are often uncertain how to behave in a novel situation. They are alert to any clue which their children may give. They are on the lookout for the way children are feeling, thinking and learning. They adjust their own behaviour towards the child on the basis of those clues. They may check them against the advice given in books, on television and radio, and by social workers. It is often not difficult to see who is bringing up whom in a family with a new baby. The child is not only at the centre of attention, but is continually initiating behaviour in the adults.
>
> (Shipman, 1972)

This approach to child-rearing found its fullest expression in handbooks of child-care in the forties and fifties, most notably by Dr Benjamin Spock. The techniques and ideology are rooted in ideas of individual autonomy and self-control, but they also allow for the emergence of conflict and opposition to parents and teachers – a theme we shall return to later in this chapter and in the subsequent chapters on the school.

Is the family in decline?

The model of the family so far presented is that idealised by the ad-men – father, mother and two children, but in the last 20 years there have been unprecedented changes to this traditional family image. Cohabitation and divorce have fundamentally changed the nature of family life with concomitant consequences for the nature and quality of relationships. The cornerstone of the traditional family is marriage but powerful demographic and social trends challenge those traditional notions of family life.

Although marriage is still popular with the majority of adults many are marrying later. The average age at marriage for both men and women has increased by about 2 years since the early 1970s, to just over 23 for women and 25 for men. This has resulted in a significant increase in the proportion of single men and women – among women aged 25–9 years almost a third remained unmarried in 1987 compared with just 13 per cent in 1971. As marriage rates declined over the last two decades cohabitation increased in popularity. 'Cohabitation before marriage is now virtually typical. This was true for 48% of women married in 1987 against just 7% in the early 1970's. By the end of this decade such cohabitation will become the norm' (Wicks, 1990). More significant for our purposes is the increasing number and proportion of children born outside of marriage to cohabiting parents. The proportion of all children born outside wedlock has more than doubled in the 1980s from 12 per cent to 27 per cent; and more of these children are being registered at birth by both parents and about half of them live with cohabiting parents. The trend is European-wide – as is the increase in the number of divorces. In Britain approximately 37 per cent of new marriages will end in divorce and the average length of marriages is 15 years.

The above trends mean that a high proportion of the children in our schools spend part of their early lives in families that are very different from the conventional model. The increase in the number of children born outside marriage together with high rates of marital breakdown has led to a significant increase in the number of one-parent families. Today 16 per cent of all dependent children live with one parent – in nine out of ten cases their mother. In 1971 the figure was 8 per cent.

> The reconstituted, or step, family is also growing in importance. Substantial proportions of divorced people eventually remarry, particularly men. For example, among men who divorced during the period 1977–1980, almost three quarters (72%) had remarried within five years. However, more and more step-families are based on cohabitation, not remarriage. Probably about one in 10 children in Britain today live in step-families, normally with their own mother and a step-father.
>
> (Wicks, 1990)

In addition to the changes described in the above paragraph you may wish to consider some of the other reasons given for the so-called decline of the family – and maybe, add some of your own.

(1) The breakdown of the extended family (including grandparents, aunts, uncles etc. living in close proximity and in regular contact) to be replaced with the *nuclear family* (husband, wife and children) as a consequence of greater social and geographic mobility.

(2) A change in the status of women so that they are looking for more in marriage – closer relationships, shared roles and responsibilities, and a greater unwillingness to 'put up with things'.

(3) More women go out to work so that the modern two-parent family is increasingly a dual-worker family.

(4) The boundaries and sanctity of marriage are being rejected with increases in pre- and extra-marital sex.

(5) The family has less influence over its members – other agencies such as schools, peer groups and the mass media have increased influence.

(6) Legislation on divorce, homosexuality and abortion has modified society's perception of conventional family life and child-rearing.

The changes in the family described in this section clearly have implications for the nature, and in some cases, quality of relationships. Therefore, it is important that teachers have knowledge of the families of the children in their classes and approach with understanding any discussion of individual families and families in general – as in project work. Some of the issues are illustrated in the following case-study of a family well-known to the authors. Family structure has implications for a child's sense of identity.

Case-study (names have been changed)

Amy was born outside of marriage. Her mother, Sue, who was nineteen at the time, refused to have an abortion as she wanted the baby but did not want to get married to the father. She lived with her parents and unmarried sister, and as grandfather was the only male in the household Amy called him Dad – as did his two daughters. As Sue was working he took Amy to nursery school where he was regarded as her father. Amy is now four years old and Sue is engaged and cohabiting with a new boyfriend, Dave. At school Amy now tells everyone, 'I've got two Dads!' As she gets older Sue knows that her family position will have to be discussed with Amy and should the couple decide to get married her family name may become an issue to be resolved.

Primary socialisation

The approach to socialisation presented by Symbolic Interactionism is frequently referred to as the *biographical model*. This is because it is concerned with the *acquisition of selfhood* as an ongoing, reciprocal life-long process, which traces an individual's history from infancy to death (see p. 9). Each individual's history is interlocked in other people's histories and all biographies are deeply influenced by social class, family relationships, educational opportunities, work experiences and the full gamut of routine, everyday life. Thus, the acquisition of self is not a casual affair, for the infant is born into a packaged world, most of which he has to accept without question. Moreover, the role of a child is usually precisely defined, with expectations and demands not permitting much scope for individual interpretation. In other words, there is no way in which an individual can constitute himself during this formative period of early childhood.

The child is born into a family in which *primary socialisation* takes place. Within the family structure there are different role players – mother, father, other children – with whom the newborn has to learn to interact. Not only does the infant learn his own role but he also has to learn the role requirements of the other family members, that is, he has to learn to take the role of each of the others. It follows that the child's view of himself is heavily dependent on how other people respond to his behaviour. Eventually, the child begins to take the role of a much wider range of people outside the family context but into each new situation he takes a history of social experiences. It is this interplay between the historical dimension and situational dimension that results in each person's unique social self.

Thus it is during primary socialisation that the child acquires a *sense of identity* – and a *sense of location*. Central to this process of knowing who we are is the means whereby children learn that they are reflexive beings; that is, they discover that they can communicate and talk to themselves in much the same way as they can communicate and talk to other people. In other words, socialisation is the process whereby the individual becomes capable of talking to himself.

> To speak of acquisition of self is therefore to speak in the most basic sense of learning a language. The child is born into a community of speakers of a particular language, and thus is also born into a pre-existing world of objects that are embedded in vocabulary and grammar. From the child's point of view, these objects simply exist. As Alfred Lindesmith and Anselm Strauss have written, '... things have names ... and names have things'. Every act of speech in which the child participates, whether as speaker or listener, brings him or her into contact with this world of objects, and it is the child's task to discover what those objects mean. The child must not only learn the names of things, but also infer the 'things of names'.
>
> (Hewitt, 1976)

The relationship between primary socialisation and secondary socialisation is implicit in the biographical model, which presents socialisation as a life-long, continuous process. The debate amongst socialisation theorists revolves around how overwhelmingly formulative early childhood experience is seen to be. For if primary socialisation is the incubator of identity acquisition then secondary socialisation is that process whereby the child learns to cope with and internalise the role expectations of the wider world. From this perspective,

> secondary socialisation builds upon the role identification of childhood. In the first instance, this is done through the direct influence of the school which is supposed to take over from the family. The school provides a cognitive framework in which the child is presumed to acquire the intellectual and social skills necessary for later life.
>
> (Open University, D207, 1980)

In the following pages we will consider two aspects of primary socialisation, namely, language acquisition, because of its centrality to the SI approach and, discipline, as this is important to how well the child accommodates to being a pupil.

Language at home and school

Most children have acquired a basic mastery of their mother tongue long before they start school. Furthermore, parents are very much their children's teachers, even though they may never think of themselves as such, or be aware of the strategies they use to help children acquire language. At the same time, language skills have a central place in school learning, as the medium of instruction through which teachers explain and direct, and children report observations and express ideas.

In the previous chapter we presented the idea that language shapes our thinking, and in recent decades educationalists have examined the notion that language might even define the limits of our learning. Pre-eminent in this field has been Basil Bernstein who, since the 1950s, has been concerned with studies that make links between social structure and educational attainment through analyses of language. Bernstein distinguishes between linguistic codes – the *restricted* and the *elaborated*. Briefly expressed, the restricted code is a form of speech that can be predicted by the observer; it usually involves short, simple sentences where the speech is descriptive and narrative rather than analytic and abstract; it focuses upon concrete items and contains implicit meanings; and the manner and circumstances of speech are of importance as well as content. In contrast, the elaborated code consists of much more explicit meanings, is difficult to predict, and is analytic and abstract. Moreover, extra-verbal factors are of little importance to it.

In Bernstein's view, these two linguistic codes are linked to patterns of socialisation between the social classes, whereby the normative system of the middle class gives rise to the use of elaborated code speech variants, while the working class child is socialised into using restricted code speech variants. Though Bernstein does add the following modifying caveat that:

> children socialized within middle class and associated strata can be expected to possess both an elaborated and a restricted code while children socialized within some sections of the working class structure,

particularly the lower working class, can be expected to be limited to a restricted code. As a child progresses through a school it becomes critical for him to possess, or at least to be oriented toward, an elaborated code if he is to succeed.

(Bernstein, 1970a)

Of key importance to the theory is the way in which meanings are articulated through language. Bernstein argues that intimate social relationships, including those within the family, community and workplace, are based on shared contexts and similar experiences, and thus communication can take place with a relatively restricted code. He argues that where such 'closed' settings and relationships exist 'it is plausible to assume that such social settings will generate a particular form of communication which will shape the intellectual, social and affective orientation of the children.' The resulting form of communication will 'emphasise verbally the communal rather than the abstract, substance rather than the elaboration of processes, the here and now rather than the explanation of motives and intentions' (Bernstein, 1970a). On the other hand, talk in school often involves communicating ideas and feelings that are outside the shared experience and understanding of participants, so that meanings have to be made explicit in a relatively elaborated use of language. Thus Bernstein argues that children whose life style requires them to be adept at using an elaborated code are at an advantage in terms of participating in school learning.

However, Bernstein does not leave his analysis at social class, as he subsequently argued that 'as the connection between social class and linguistic codes is too imprecise' it is necessary to distinguish between two ideal types of family role systems – *positional* and *person-oriented families*. In positional families decisions are made according to the formal status of a person's role (father, mother, child). Such a family system gives rise to 'closed' communications which is less likely to encourage the verbalisation of individual differences, intentions and motives, since they are prescribed by the family. Social control relies upon the relative power of the people involved rather than on speech. By comparison, person-oriented families occur where decisions are made on the grounds of psychological and individual differences of members; and 'open' communication encourages discussion and the expression of their individual differences by members of the family. In these instances social control is exercised more through verbal elaboration and relies less upon formal status and power.

Broadly, he argues that there is a relationship between the working class, positional family and the restricted code and the middle class, person-oriented family and the elaborated code. However, he does add that some working class families are more person-oriented, and that the middle class has access to both codes. In general terms, *all* people have access to restricted codes, but parts of the working class do not have the same access to an elaborated code as do the middle class.

> It happens, however, that this communication code (restricted) directs the child to orders of learning and relevance that are not in harmony with those required by the school. Where the child is sensitive to the communication system of the school and thus to its orders of learning and relation, then the experience of school for this child is not sensitive . . . then this child's experience . . . becomes one of symbolic and social change. In the first case we have an elaboration of social identity; in the second case, a change of social identity. Thus between the school and community of the working-class child, there may exist a cultural discontinuity upon two radically different systems of communication.
>
> (Bernstein, 1971)

Bernstein's work, whilst attempting to provide an explanation of the link between social structure and educational attainment through language, is controversial. Some critics have argued that the code thesis has contributed to the relatively common view that the language and thought of the 'lower' classes suffers from verbal deprivation. William Labov's work with lower-class negro children in the US can be singled out as having achieved most in terms of dispelling the myth of the language deficient home by demonstrating that these children are not inarticulate, and that their speech is logical, grammatical and expressive, although different from standard American English (Labov, 1969). In fairness to Bernstein, he too recognised differences rather than deficiencies and argued that we should lay less emphasis on the ability of the child to adjust to the school, and more on the requirement that the teacher adjusts the curriculum and teaching to the cultural and linguistic mix in the classroom. In criticising compensatory education (Bernstein, 1970b) he held, 'If the culture of the teacher is to become part of the consciousness of the child, then the culture of the child must first be in the consciousness of the teacher.' At the beginning of this chapter a similar sentiment was expressed with reference to the personal and social education. One of the problems is the teacher's relative ignorance about the home life of the children they teach.

Discipline and social control

In the section on language the work of Bernstein also focused on the nature of authority relations within family structure – positional and person-oriented. The pattern of discipline exercised in the home will not only have a bearing on the child's behaviour within the family but also in secondary contexts, such as, the school, clubs and organisations, and even around the streets. It will influence their relations with other children and their responses to authority figures, such as, teacher, brownie/cub leaders, and even the police. In this discussion of discipline we shall look at some general models of parental control and children's social behaviour, and then look at an influential longitudinal study carried out by John and Elizabeth Newson.

In a summary of child-rearing practices Schaefer (1959) produced the following figure (2). The horizontal axis is *affection*, which ranges from hostility to loving, whilst the vertical axis focuses on degrees of *control*, which range from permissive to authoritarian. Bringing up a child is not easy and parents agonise as they restrict their child's excesses. They do not wish to be too lenient nor scolding all the time. They wish to be consistent but children can be quite cagey about pleading with or defying their parents.

In a later study of disciplinary styles Baumrind (1971) presents three distinct patterns of discipline and their bearing on children's behaviour. This study found that the three styles were consistently related to the children's social behaviour at home, in nursery school and in the laboratory

Authoritarian parents are those she found to be firm, punitive, unaffectionate and unsympathetic. They value obedience from their children and authority for themselves. They do not encourage independence and seldom give praise. Their children were found to be unfriendly, discontented, distrustful or withdrawn. At home they are given few rights but are expected to assume as much responsibility as adults.

Permissive parents in contrast do not feel in control and do not exert control. They give the child considerable freedom. Mother is loving, father is lax and ineffectual. Children in these families have few responsibilities but the same rights as adults. Their children were

Fig. 2: Alternative child-rearing patterns

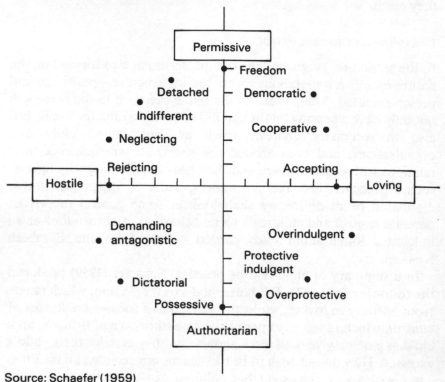

Source: Schaefer (1959)

immature, dependent, unhappy, least self-reliant or self-controlled. At home permissive parents let their children make their own decisions with few guidelines, regulations or strictures.

Authoritative (or democratic) parents view the rights and duties of parents and children as complementary. As their children mature they gradually allow them responsibility for their own behaviour. They reason with their children, encourage give and take, and listen to objections. These parents are firm and consistent, but they are also loving and understanding. They set limits, but also encourage independence. It is evident that these children are given a clear idea of what is expected of them but control is exercised in a loving framework. Such children were friendly, cooperative, self-reliant, independent, happy and socially responsible.

One may raise objections to such broad disciplinary styles and for our own purposes question whether they have any long-term effects on children's behaviour into adolescence. Consistent with our theses of

Table 1: Actual smacking frequency reported by mothers (in percentages)

	Social class					Summary		
(a) At least once a week	I and II	III (wc)	III (man)	IV	V	Middle class	Working class	Overall popn
Boys %	39	47	54	52	63	43	55	52
Girls %	18	26	33	27	49	22	33	30
Both %	29	36	43	39	56	32	44	41

Significance: trend ↗ ****   m.class/w. class**

between sexes****

(b) Less than once a month								
Boys %	35	22	23	26	19	29	23	25
Girls %	52	43	34	38	28	48	34	38
Both %	44	33	29	32	24	38	29	31

Significance: trend ↘ ***   m.class/w.class**

between sexes ****

Source: Newson and Newson (1976)

interactive socialisation we must recognise the two-way nature of any control strategies and that the child will influence the effectiveness of parents' disciplinary styles.

The Newsons' research data comes from a running sample of 700 families in Nottingham whose mothers were interviewed in depth in their own homes, as the children reached their first, fourth, seventh, eleventh and sixteenth birthdays. These children are now in their twenties and many have children of their own. Most of the illustrative material is from *Seven Years Old in the Home Environment* (Newson and Newson, 1976), as seven is the age when parent control plays an important part in a child's life and particularly as he begins to assert himself as a person in his own right in other social contexts like school.

We shall concentrate on physical punishment for two reasons. Firstly, because it is the form of control we most often associate with punishment for wrong doings by this age group and, secondly, because of the recent attention given to the physical abuse of children. Table 1 shows the incidence of smacking as reported by Nottingham mothers.

One should interpret the data to see what trends emerge. For example, 41 per cent of the sample appear to use smacking routinely as a way of punishment, whilst 31 per cent resort to it infrequently, if at all. The incidence of physical punishment is related to social class and

Table 2: Acceptance of punishment principle as a function of social class and the child's sex (in percentages)

| | Social class | | | | | | Summary | |
	I and II	III (wc)	III (man)	IV	V	Middle class	Working class	Overall popn
High scorers (7–13)								
Boys %	25	28	37	31	39	26	36	33
Girls %	20	18	25	19	38	19	25	24
Both %	22	23	31	25	39	23	31	28

Significance: trend ↗ **   m.class/w. class*

between sexes***

Low scorers (0–3)								
Boys %	29	21	22	21	16	25	21	22
Girls %	38	35	16	29	26	37	20	24
Both %	34	28	19	25	21	31	20	23

Significance: trend ↘ **   m.class/w.class***

between sexes n.s.

Source: Newson and Newson (1976)

there is a marked difference between the figure for boys and girls. Does this mean that girls are better behaved than boys or do the figures reflect cultural attitudes?

Table 2 shows the proportion of mothers who were classified as high scorers or low scorers on an 'Index of mothers' acceptance of the 'punishment principle'. It is another attempt to distinguish between two styles of family control – democratic and authoritarian. A high score is considered to be indicative of a belief in the parent's right to use punishment to establish control, and a low score of belief in the establishment of internal control through democratic means.

Once again there are social class and sex differences. Middle-class mothers are apparently less likely to believe in punishment as a necessary or effective principle, and are less likely to practise an authoritarian style of discipline than working-class mothers. From elsewhere in the study we also learn of the cumulative use of different forms of punishment. In summary, the more often a mother smacks, the more likely she is to use deprivation punishment as well.

Although one is cautious about drawing too strict a dichotomy between social class differences the evidence does suggest that middle-class parents are more likely to emphasise *verbal elaboration* as they

Table 3: 'Bamboozlers' and 'non-bamboozlers' analysed by social class and the child's sex (in percentages)

	Social class						Summary	
	I and II	III (wc)	III (man)	IV	V	Middle class	Working class	Overall popn
Bamboozlement score								
Zero:								
Boys %	71	46	33	31	14	59	31	38
Girls %	65	51	35	29	28	58	33	40
Both %	68	48	34	30	21	58	32	39

Significance: trend ↘ ＊＊＊＊ m.class/w. class＊＊＊＊

between sexes n.s.

	I and II	III (wc)	III (man)	IV	V	Middle class	Working class	Overall popn
2 or more:								
Boys %	15	25	30	40	46	20	34	30
Girls %	8	14	34	39	33	11	35	28
Both %	11	20	32	39	39	15	34	29

Significance: trend ↘ ＊＊＊＊ m.class/w.class＊＊＊＊

between sexes n.s.

Source: Newson and Newson (1976)

rationalise the issues and emphasise the moral implication of their action to the child. In fact, the Newsons argue that verbal elaboration is reflected in social class differences in other aspects of the way language is used, for example, when a threat is used to deprive a child of sweets or TV, or to send him early to bed. The Newsons interpret this as follows:

> We would relate this to the strong value placed by middle-class mothers upon words as the agents of truth which we noted when the children were four, that is, once an idea is formulated in words, this invests it with substance which must not then be negated. Thus it is an integral part of the middle-class philosophy that a threat should only be put into words if parents are also prepared to carry it through into action . . .
> Working-class mothers, and in particular lower-working-class mothers, are on the other hand rather more likely to be prepared to use words, as expedients for short-term aims, with less pernickety regard for their content in terms of truth.
>
> (Newson and Newson, 1976)

To this data on short-term threats the Newsons add further evidence on mothers' willingness to deceive in other ways – threatening with the police, threats to leave home, threats to withdraw love – which they label 'bamboozlement'. Table 3 shows the proportions of social class groups who score high and low on their index. High scores indicate a greater use of bamboozlement. In other words, there appears to be class-related differences in how important parents feel truth to be when disciplining their children.

> These figures support those we presented at four on mothers' willingness to 'evade or distort the truth'. We speculated then that, because the mother is likely to set the pattern for a child's later attitudes towards authority, her willingness to use bluff and bamboozlement may sow the seeds of distrust of later authorities, such as teachers in the first instance and the agencies of law and administration later on. It is as true at seven as it was at four that 'the most widely used [disciplinary] deception in Class V is the idle threat of authorities outside the home ... so that many children must initially meet these personages as allies of an angry mother, whose own falseness they must soon discover'. Since mothers are only intermittently angry, however, we particularly questioned the effects of the child coming to realise, as he inevitably must, that it is a supposedly benevolent authority who has deliberately used trickery in her dealing with him: this one might expect to have a more subtly powerful influence than would deception from a frankly malevolent source. These findings do not yet give us any firm answers; but they do make us feel that continued conjecture in this vein is more than justified.
>
> (Newson and Newson, 1976)

In conclusion, the Newsons (1989) have found no reason to suppose that the extent of parental punishment has decreased across the social class board. In 1958, 62 per cent of mothers indicated that they smacked their one-year-old babies, in the 1985 sample 63 per cent of mothers said they smacked their one year old.

There is an organisation called EPOCH (End Physical Punishment of Children) which maintains that smacking is a short-cut to nowhere.

> The difference between 'reasonable punishment' and 'cruel abuse' is only a matter of degree. It's a thin line and, wherever you choose to draw the line in your family, it is easily overstepped.
>
> (Leach, 1989)

In the following chapter we discuss the major transfer from home to school. How a child will settle into pupilhood will depend on how well they have been prepared for school so that there is a continuity of experiences. A smooth transition makes the adjustment to school demands less traumatic and lays the foundation for continuing enjoyment of school and successful achievement. Integrated children, who are compatible with teacher expectations and have a sense of what is appropriate, provide complimentary role partners, thus making the teacher's job pleasant. They facilitate a harmonious classroom atmosphere for all children as developing 'centres of consciousness' (Peters, 1966).

Exercises

(1) In an educational climate in which the education press and staffrooms are preoccupied with the National Curriculum, assessment, test results etc., how relevant is it for us to discuss the educative role of the family?

(2) Complete Cohen and Cohen's semantic differential scale (p. 29) and check to what extent your group agrees with their findings. Then discuss whether you think that teachers will differently perceive their role in the light of recent government legislation.

(3) To what extent do you agree with the view that the teaching of literacy and numeracy should be left to the experts, as it requires specialist training and therefore is beyond the comprehension of parents?

(4) Consider this quotation from EPOCH (Leach, 1989), 'Smacking has to be wrong because we all agree that hitting people is wrong and children are people – aren't they?'. Where do you stand on this issue?

Additional reading

1. Leach, P. (1989) 'Smacking – a short cut to nowhere', EPOCH, London, is a booklet in which the arguments against smacking are fully developed.
2. Keirnan, K. and Wicks, M. (1990) *Family Changes and Future Policy*, The Family Policy Studies Centre, London, discusses the changes in family life in greater detail.

CHAPTER 3

Socialisation and the Concept of Pupil Career

Home to school

Progress from home to compulsory schooling is an event that is significant for children, for whom it means new experiences and new relationships. It is also significant for parents as they first accompany their children to school and hand over responsibility for at least part of their children's child-rearing to a professional person and a formal organisation. For this reason, progress into pupilhood at around five years of age has been called a form of social weaning. For upon entering the school for the first time the child meets a whole set of new constraints – new ways of behaving, new forms of authority, and new methods of evaluation. The child must adapt to the demands made by fresh surroundings, relationships, timetabled work and play, and a whole range of behavioural expectations. And even though many children now have the opportunity to go to some form of pre-schooling the actual entry into the infant class can still be upsetting for many.

As we noted in the previous chapter, a great deal of social learning has already taken place in the family setting but upon entry into school more formal education takes place. One of the functions of the school is to socialise children into the 'ways of society', that is, to give the child the knowledge and skills necessary for survival in an advanced industrial society. This process, though, extends beyond literacy and numeracy, to include beliefs, attitudes, habits and appropriate normative behaviour. In addition, and even as a pre-requisite to teaching the ways of society, it is necessary that the neophyte be socialised into the ways of the school – its routines, rules and rituals. This is the child's entry into pupilhood and the importance of a successful introduction into the new role will be evident to all who work with children and young people.

51

But a successful entry into pupilhood is not just about learning the ways of the school, it also involves striking up a relationship with the first teacher. The establishment of a good relationship is a most important first step in the socialising process of the school. For, from the point of view of the child, how happily he settles will greatly influence how successful he becomes and will largely shape the course of his future school career. Relationships with the first teacher are partly dependent upon the experience of relationships with parents, or with other adults, which the child has had at home and in the wider community. The degree of ease of assimilating into the socialising process of the school and hence the child's reaction to the experience, will be powerfully influenced by the manner in which parents have prepared the child for school. Children who have received a democratic form of discipline, experienced forms of communication like those in school, and who have enjoyed pre-schooling hours away from mother, are going to fit into the demands of the infant classroom much more readily.

In this introduction we have briefly touched on the symbolic interactionist's twin concerns of social context and social relationships, and in the rest of the chapter we shall further examine their impact on a child's social self-awareness. Most teachers are familiar with the arguments about the connection between social class and school success, that is, origins and destinations in personal, social and vocational terms. Many teachers also believe that this awareness enables them to overcome the bias which knowledge of the child's social class may otherwise create, but research by interactionists has exposed the problems inherent in the teacher–pupil relationship. It is their focus upon the relationships that actually exist between child and teacher which suggest that it is the teacher's analysis of and reactions to the child, which serve to dispose that child to success or failure. Thus, it is the nature and quality of teacher-pupil interaction and their influence upon a child's social self which will strongly influence the work in this and subsequent chapters.

From childhood into pupilhood

Pupilhood is a specific phase of childhood and for most children it lasts for about eleven years (see Fig. 3). It is associated with secondary socialisation as the young child learns to cope with and internalise the role expectations of the wider outside world. Entering school means the beginning of a new career and the giving of a new status within the emerging biography of the individual. And although the sub-heading 'from childhood into pupilhood' may seem to imply a gradual progression in which the latter status is dispensed with, this is clearly not the case. Rather, it refers to a continuing process of socialisation which we move through as individuals or in groups. And despite the fact that we have presented it as an ongoing process we recognise that there are also discontinuities in the experience. For the new pupil, the continuity–discontinuity dialogue can be illustrated by considering what the new status actually means in social terms.

Continuity exists in the way schools maintain the *socially confirmed statuses* of age and sex. In other words, what happens in school is comparable with treatment at home. Boys and girls are treated differently in such fundamentals as names, dress, toys and role expectations; whilst age brings privileges and responsibilities, like which TV programmes you may watch and putting away your toys.

Discontinuity occurs (for some pupils) in school as a new *socially conferred status* is experienced, based on ability and attainment – for evaluation is a fundamental feature of schooling. A child's achievements at school become a growing preoccupation of adults both in school and in the family. For some children this aspect of their new status will be painful, frustrating and embarrassing.

In SI there is an attempt to handle the problem of continuity and discontinuity within the concept of career. The notion does not refer only to the development of an individual's occupational career but, as presented here, in a broader sense to describe 'any social strand of any person's course through life' (Goffman, 1968). The concept is particularly useful for us as it brings together both the 'objective' features of an individual's experience, the sequence of situations he is confronted by and the 'subjective' interpretation of, and adjustment to, these situations. The objective fact is that school attendance is compulsory and the setting of schooling is distinctive and very different from home. Upon facing these new situations each child will seek to give them meaning and, with varying degrees of success, adjust to them. And, as we have already noted, some children may be persuaded to adjust to an unfavourable self-definition – and with what consequences for his self-concept and subsequent behaviour?

> Traditionally the term career has been reserved for those who expect to enjoy the rises laid out within a respectable profession. The term is coming to be used, however, in a broadened sense to refer to any social strand of any person's course through life . . . One value of the concept career is its two-sidedness. One side is linked to internal matters held

dearly and closely...the other side concerns public position, jural relations, and style of life... The concept of career, then, allows one to move back and forth between the personal and public, between the self and its significant society... The main concern will be with the moral aspects of career – that is, the regular sequence of changes that career entails in the person's self and in his framework of imagery for judging himself and others.

(Goffman, 1968)

Much of what has been written on career has focused on deviant careers. For example, Goffman (1968) describes the 'moral career of the mental patient' and traces the process by which an individual becomes *labelled* as mentally ill and in need of treatment. The change of status involved here is from being regarded as 'normal' by others and capable of independent action to being classified as 'abnormal' and in need of specialised help. Once the individual has been admitted to hospital he has to accommodate a new situation, both in terms of physical surroundings and social relationships, involving the whole process of *situational adjustment* and the achieving of a new identity. Only when a shared set of meanings exist between himself, other patients and hospital staff can this particular 're-socialisation' process be regarded as complete.

During life we make many situational adjustments, most very small, but some major ones, like starting work, getting married, retirement, entering hospital. For a child, starting school is probably the most challenging adjustment (see Fig. 3). Linked with the concept of situational adjustment is *anticipatory socialisation* and also, *status passage*. Transition from home to school can be upsetting, even traumatic, for a child. The child leaves a warm, intimate, familiar place for a large, confusing, strange place. How well that transition is effected can determine the child's acceptance of school and all that it offers and represents. It is for this reason that we need to carefully look at status passages within education and examine how we can smooth the path of transition. For those early experiences can have a major bearing on a pupil's subsequent career. In this chapter we will look at two periods of transition – starting school and transfer from primary to secondary school.

In schools there are those careers which are officially fostered and sanctioned and those which are discouraged and forbidden. We shall start by looking at the officially approved careers and then look in detail at disapproved careers, such as, disrupter and truant. An important consideration must be the relationship between social

Fig. 3: Becoming a pupil

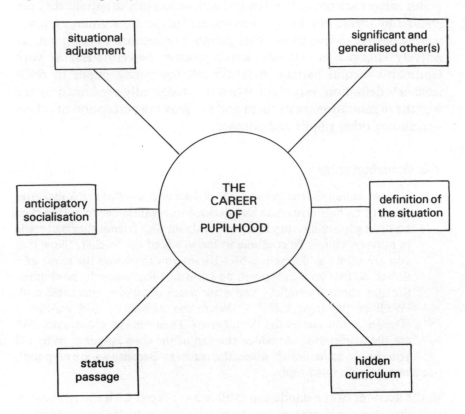

situations and self-identities, that is, to what extent the school's organisation actually contributes to the development of those careers which itself condemns.

The officially sanctioned careers are closely linked to the newly conferred status of pupilhood. They are experienced through the maze of knowledge and behaviour contained within the formal and informal curriculum, timetabling and rules as presented and interpreted by teachers. The culmination of successful, officially approved careers are celebrated by top table, gold stars, monitorships and the awarding of prizes. In addition, the school also approves of other successful channels, notably, sporting success and participation in a range of functions, such as, morning assembly, plays and concerts, clubs and outside activities. However, there is evidence that there is a fairly high correlation between academic success and involvement in other activities – although it is policy in most primary schools to involve as many children as possible, even if in minor parts.

But careers are not only *given* to participants in a situation, they are *created* by them. For human beings, no matter how young, are not merely passive recipients of other people's definitions of them but are actively engaged in the interactive process. Nevertheless, as with Goffman's mental patient, it is difficult for young pupils to resist teacher's definition, especially when it is repeatedly confirmed by the way the organisation treats them and the growing perception of others – including other pupils and parents.

The dandelion table

Here we include a true story told by a teacher at a coffee break just after the autumn half-term. She had decided to organise her reception class according to ability, they had previously sat with friends they had made in nursery school. To continue in the words of the teacher, 'Now that you are sitting at different tables I want you to choose the name of a flower, so that your group will be known by that name.' The children thought about it carefully and after much discussion one table said, 'We'll be the Rose table' – 'We're the daffodils', said another – 'Daisies', volunteered the third group. Then the last group said, 'We are the dandelions.' At which the rest of the class laughed. 'Why did you choose dandelions?' asked the teacher. 'Because we are no good', was their very sad reply.

In the account of the dandelion table we are faced with the realisation that situational adjustment can be a collective as well as an individual experience as groups develop a corporate identity. This collective awareness can either support or reject the organisation's culture. Two significant British studies of the formation of a group identity were by Hargreaves (1967) and Lacey (1970) and, although they are based in secondary schools their findings are equally important for primary schools. Hargreaves' study concentrates on the fourth year pupils in a boys' secondary modern school and he saw the four streams in the years as forming the basis of informal groupings. By the process of promotion and demotion, over the years, each form developed its own norms of behaviour, and the process of conformity and deviation reflected that attitude towards the school's culture. He found that the higher the stream the greater the tendency for a boy to be committed to the school. Higher stream pupils attended more regularly, wore school uniform, participated in school activities – they also liked school and the teachers. Their high status correlated positively with their academic achievement and good behaviour. In the lower streams the boys reversed the approved standards and displayed a negative orientation to the school's values. Top class boys approved of the teachers' conception of what their pupil role should be but in the lower classes they rejected the teachers' definition of their roles and were critical of those who met teachers' definition of pupilhood. These differences were so great that Hargreaves divided the fourth year into two sub-cultures, which he called the 'academic' and the 'delinquescent'. The academic were oriented to school values and the delinquescent to extra-school values. The point to note from Hargreaves' work is that by fostering certain career lines and discouraging others, and by dividing the pupils into groups on the basis of adherence to their career lines, the school is providing both the impetus towards the creation of competing career lines and the personnel to follow them. And whilst Hargreaves is describing adolescent boys we are sure that many primary school teachers will recognise the beginnings of an anti-school attitude in some of their year five and year six pupils and predict problem times for them upon transfer to the local secondary school.

Lacey's study picks up this latter point of what happened to boys when they transfer to the local grammar school. At the beginning of their grammar school career, this highly selected, relatively homogeneous group, show a strong commitment to the values of the school. They are eager, competitive and cooperative. But upon entry a process of evaluation begins which results in 'the separation and ranking of students according to a multiple set of criteria which makes up the normative, academically oriented, value system of the grammar school' (Lacey, 1970). This he calls *differentiation* and is largely carried out by teachers. The consequence of differentiation is *polarisation*, which is a pupil initiated, sub-culture formation to which the school-dominated, normative culture is opposed. But there are casualties in this process, as eleven-year-old boys who have been 'best pupils' in their primary schools try to come to terms with the redefinition of their pupil status. They had been 'best pupils' for some time and internalised many of the expectations and personal self-awareness inherent in that position.

> Their transfer to grammar school means not only a new environment, with all that such a change entails – new classmates, new teacher and new sets of rules – but also for many of them a violation of their expectation as 'best pupils'. It is when this violation of expectation

coincides with 'unsatisfactory' home backgrounds that the worst cases of emotional disturbance occur.

(Lacey, 1970)

Lacey records the following list of fifteen cases of major disturbances, although there was probably a larger number of minor ones which never became known to the school.

Bursting into tears when reprimanded by a teacher.
Refusal to go to school or to particular lessons, accompanied by hysterical crying and screaming.
Sleeplessness.
Bedwetting.
Playing truant from certain lessons or from school.
Constantly feeling sick before certain lessons.
One boy rushed to the stage in assembly clutching his throat and screaming that he could not breathe.
Consistent failure to do homework.
High absence record.
Aggravation of mild epilepsy.

(Lacey, 1970)

Critical stages in a pupil's career

Starting school

Starting school is a vital step in a child's personal and social development and for this reason alone should be thoughtfully planned and prepared for. In their report AMMA (1987) identify the following that children need to learn, know and use as 'survival skills' in a classroom.

- who they are and what they can do;
- that 'experience' has some meaning for them;
- that they have a right to their own interests and knowledge;
- what school is for, and what it is in physical terms;
- how to be with, consider and communicate with other adults and children when necessary;
- who teachers and other adults in school are and what they are for;
- how to help themselves in activities such as taking coats off, going to the lavatory or organising themselves in a chosen activity;
- how to cope with and overcome 'not knowing' things and the feelings this arouses.

Not knowing any of these (but particularly the first and last) leads to children feeling uncertain, out of control and apparently confused. At the extreme their responses are difficult to cope with in large classes but frequently (initially at least) related to confusion rather than 'bad' behaviour. Knowing the above depended on experience, expectations and opportunity to learn and practice them.

(AMMA, 1987)

Linked to the smoothness of status passage is *anticipatory socialisation*, the process whereby an individual adopts the attitudes of a group to which he does not yet belong – the professional socialisation of teachers is an illustration. The more effectively it is carried out the smoother the transition into the new status. Some children learn about school from older children in the family but some form of pre-school education is undoubtedly the best method of preparation. The importance of the provision of nursery-type education lies not so much in lasting academic gains but in personal and social advantages. It prepares children for full-time schooling by gradually adjusting them to being with other children, responding to relative strangers who have charge of them, and experiencing being in an orderly, controlled environment.

Since the Plowden Report (1967) the importance of parental involvement has been highlighted and given official recognition. The provisions of the Education Acts of 1980, 1981, 1986 and 1988 allow parental views considerable weight and so successful home–school links have become more formally sanctioned. First contacts between home and school need to be handled sensitively and thoughtfully to assist the transition stage and also to lay secure foundations for future parental involvement. The methods adopted by schools will vary but are likely to include one or more of the following:

(1) Parents are invited to visit the school in the term prior to admission – often at an informal gathering to acquaint parents with the organisation of the school, to get to know the head-teacher, class teacher and each other.

(2) On the first day parents are invited to stay with the children in the classroom but the visit is kept relatively short so that the children are not overwhelmed or over-tired and leave happy and settled.

(3) Some headteachers or nursery/reception class teachers make home visits to new entrants.

(4) An extention of this contact, to be found in some LEAs, is the appointment of home–school liaison teachers whose role is to

prepare parents and children for the transition. In examples 3 and 4 it is a good idea for the contact to take information booklets, story books and a specially prepared pack of learning materials.

(5) Many schools adopt a staggered admission system over a week and operate vertical grouping or family grouping where older children help the new ones settle in and provide good models.

(6) Another interesting introduction in a small number of schools is to use any spare room as a parents' room, where they can meet and talk to the class teacher and work together should they be involved as volunteer helpers.

But a classroom is also a very busy, active place into which the teacher must bring some order and it is in response to this contextual demand that teachers exercise their authority and children are expected to comply. The initiative in classroom interaction rests with the teacher and one only has to observe a reception class at the beginning and end of a term to appreciate the amount of social learning that has taken place.

Transfer from primary to secondary school

Compared with our rising-five children the pupils who transfer to secondary school have already spent more than six years, which is over half of their compulsory schooling, in a primary school. Therefore, they are familiar with many of the general features of schools and teachers. Nevertheless, this is still a major adjustment and they face it with a mixture of excitement and apprehension. They are hesitant about leaving the familiar small school for the much larger secondary, even though they look forward to the challenge of new subjects, special facilities and going to the 'big school' –with all that that means. Most children settle into their new school without too much fuss – but this does not mean that they don't have worries. Those who do have worries can be unhappy and unsuccessful, for these early experiences can adversely affect a pupil's subsequent career. The seeds of under-achievement and disaffection are sown during this critical transfer.

Good schools, that is, secondaries and their feeder primaries, are aware of the importance of this transition and in cooperation devise a preparatory and settling in programme. Their aims should be :

(1) to remove anxiety and ensure that the initial eager anticipation is sustained, and

(2) to maintain both continuity and momentum in pupils' work and achievement.

Fig. 4: Anxieties about transfer

Galton and Willcocks (1983)	Hamblin (1978)	Youngman and Lunzer (1977)	Davies (1986)	Measor and Woods (1984) (from middle school)
Bullying	Homework	Things stolen	Bullying	Size of school
Separation from friends	Examinations	Losing things	Specific subjects	New work demands
Size of school	New teachers	School work	Getting lost	Losing friends
	Bullying	Examinations	Homework	Bullying
	Size of school	Bullying		New forms of discipline and authority

The methods adopted to achieve these aims will vary from school to school but in every case they should direct their induction programmes towards alleviating the concerns commonly expressed in research surveys into pupil transfer (Fig. 4 lists some research findings).

To give substance to the lists in Fig. 4 we offer extracts from a survey carried out by the authors on behalf of one comprehensive and its eight feeder schools. An open-ended questionnaire was completed by the pupils immediately after the Autumn half-term of their first year. It was aimed at finding out how well the youngsters had settled into their new school and to what extent their hopes and fears had been realised. Most were happy and enjoying the new experience. Christopher's answer is typical:

> Yes I have enjoyed my first few weeks at the comprehensive because I enjoy the subjects we have to do and the teachers are very nice and the facilities are very good.
>
> Christopher

On the other hand, the rest of the quotations have been chosen to convey the kinds of worries the pupils continued to have even after six weeks.

Practical problems

> ... has been different to what I expected it to be because it is much more rushed than my old school.
>
> Alexander

> The day seems much longer in this school than in my other.
>
> Rosalyn

Getting on the bus worries me because everyone starts to push you.

Julie

It isn't really quite what I had expected. My Dad said that I would be surprised at the dinners. I was surprised, the queue was terreble.

Steven

I have found the biggest difference in the cuing up for dinners.

Amanda

Strict teachers

I have enjoyed some subjects. I realy did not like 600 lines.

Simon

Well the night I had to do 600 lines the next day I was bard so I thought the teachers might think I was mitchen [truanting] because of the lines.

Simon

No I havent because Im always geting told of when I havent don enything to anoy the teacher and I dont enjoy it because of some of the teachers.

Mark

Forgetting equipment

I always worry about forgetting my books and getting detention for it. My mother would be very annoyed. And today I forgot my Welsh Book. So I am worried what she'll [Welsh teacher] say.

Jane

Bullying

I enjoy school except for one or two boys who are very unpleasant.

Andrew

Short and long-term measures

To help pupils with what is a critical adjustment in their pupil career schools need to devise both short-term and long-term measures along the following lines.

Short-term measures depend upon close liaison between the receiving secondary school and the feeder primaries.

(1) Many schools have a twelve month induction programme to get the youngsters to gradually identify with their new school. It will include many of the measures listed under 3 below.

(2) Parents must be fully involved in the programme. For they too are anxious about their child's transfer and if their worries are not allayed they will transmit them to their son or daughter. First year handbooks and general prospectus should be informative and welcoming – and not too full of teacher jargon.

(3) The structured programme should contain some of the following:

    (a) regular communications from the secondary school to the new pupils and their parents, for example, a copy of the newsletter;

    (b) at least one whole-day visit to the school during which they should meet their form tutors, class teachers, visit specialist rooms and partake in the lunchtime routine;

    (c) during the visit first formers should act as guides and information stewards;

    (d) all new pupils should be given a map of the school – some schools hold familiarisation sessions, when a 'Treasure Hunt' is organised with prizes;

    (e) specialist subject teachers should visit the feeder primaries – teacher exchanges can be very beneficial;

    (f) cooperative activities can be organised, for example, concerts, celebration of festivals;

    (g) senior staff from the receiving school should meet with parents of the new intake, preferably in the primary schools where the groups will be smaller and the meeting less formal;

    (h) every pupil should be placed in a class/tutor group with at least one friend from her/his primary school;

    (i) continuity of the curriculum must be planned to reduce discontinuities and the National Curriculum makes this even more imperative. Heads of Departments should meet and liaise with Subject Leaders;

    (j) there should be an open exchange of information.

Long-term measures in the adjustment process rest mainly with the secondary schools. They should have in place a pastoral care system which contains a programme to cater for the personal and social development of young people. Adolescence is a challenging time:

(1) It is a period of rapid personal change – physical, emotional and social – when relationships are intensely felt.
(2) Adolescence is that time between childhood and adulthood when young people are in 'search of an identity'.
(3) This is also the time when youth culture makes its greatest impact. There is a clash of cultures between youth culture and the culture of the school.

Deviant careers in schools

We have already noted earlier that much of the literature on career has focused on deviant careers. Studies in education are no different, for they too have concentrated on non-conformist behaviour, such as, disruption, truancy, vandalism and bullying. In this section we will look at the disrupter and truant but leave our discussion of the bully–victim interaction to the chapter on social education and peer relationships (Chapter 6). It will be evident that the notion of career is linked to the act of *labelling*. The importance of labelling is particularly marked when the label refers to a person as being of a particular type, as being a certain kind of person. For example, in education we label children as maladjusted, slow learners, retarded, poor readers and so on. Such labels can be applied to anyone once their behaviour has been defined in certain ways. It is also the case that the significance of attaching labels to people is influenced by the position of the person concerned. The significance is greatest when the person doing the labelling has the official authority to do so and to make the label stick. In matters to do with schooling the authority of the teachers is highly significant and it is difficult for a pupil to resist a negative label when the full authority of the education system is organised to confirm that definition.

Disruptive behaviour

Pupils can express their disaffection with school by either striking out, staying away or fading into the background. In recent years the profession has been concerned about the large number of alienated children and young people. A more detailed examination of the reasons why certain pupils adopt alternative careers will be left to subsequent chapters on social context (Chapter 4) and teacher expectations (Chapter 5). In response to expressions of concern by teacher unions, following a number of surveys which indicated an increased number of teachers had been physically or verbally abused, the Secretary of State for Education set up a Committee of Enquiry under the Chairmanship of Lord Elton. In March 1989 their report, 'Discipline in Schools', was published and, as required by its terms of reference, addressed both disruptive behaviour and absenteeism. In Tattum (1989b) there is a detailed review and critique of two decades of surveys and reports on discipline in schools from teacher unions, local authorities, HMI, plus local and individual surveys.

The Elton Report makes particular reference to the results of the Professional Association of Teachers' survey, which was in part instrumental in the setting up of the Enquiry. The survey was conducted in Autumn 1987 in conjunction with the Daily Express. Members were invited to complete a questionnaire in their professional journal and from the responses of 1,500 teachers to the question, 'Have you ever been subjected to a physical attack by a pupil?' a disturbing 32 per cent answered in the affirmative.

From a similarly worded question in an NOP survey of a controlled sample of nearly 500 NUT members only 5 per cent replied that they had been physically assaulted or threatened (*Teacher*, 1988). Consideration of the wide discrepancy in the percentages highlights the research problems and, more importantly, the influence the figures can have on public perception and professional response to the issue of indiscipline. Faced with these and other inconsistencies the Committee commissioned its own survey from Sheffield University's Educational Research Centre. The research involved a nationally representative sample of just under 3,200 secondary and 1,200 primary school teachers, and also interviews of 100 teachers in 10 inner city secondary schools not covered by the survey. Just over 2 per cent of teachers reported some form of 'physical aggression' towards themselves, either in the classroom and/or about the school. The main problem reported was the 'continuous stream of relatively minor disruptions', such as, talking out of turn, bickering and jostling, hindering other pupils and calculated idleness or work avoidance. As Lord Elton reported, 'The picture is not one of crisis, but one of continual draining stress on teachers.' To perceive of the problem thus is not to underestimate its frustrating and debilitating effect on teachers, rather it recognises the nature of the problem and points us towards positive strategies.

This general picture is supported by two influential HMI reports. In *Good Behaviour and Discipline in Schools* (1987) the reported evidence was gathered from inspections since January 1983 and supplemented from special attention given to behaviour and discipline during visits to schools in the Summer term of 1986.

> The general picture of behaviour within schools which emerges from these publications is that the overwhelming majority of schools are orderly communities in which there are good standards of behaviour and discipline; poor behaviour is unusual, and serious indiscipline a rare occurrence.
>
> (HMI, 1987)

A more detailed review of recent inspections appears in the HMI (1988) report *Secondary Schools* based on 185 maintained schools visited during 1982–86. This is an important document because it provides us with the best available, comparative data between the late 1970s and the mid 1980s, and on discipline the data does not indicate any serious deterioration in secondary schools.

> Notwithstanding the difficulties in attempting to sum up the behaviour in any school, classroom behaviour was assessed as good in 61 per cent of schools and in another 34 per cent satisfactory or better, with only 5 per cent where there were substantial difficulties. Outside the class-room, 10 per cent of schools had examples of behaviour that was less than satisfactory but 52 per cent where behaviour was good and other 38 per cent where it was at least satisfactory.
>
> (HMI, 1988)

Finally in this brief consideration of disruption as a problem two cautionary points need to be made. Firstly from research carried out by AMMA (1984), Lawrence *et al.* (1986) and Laing and Chazan (1986) there is a growing concern that the prevalence of behaviour problems is increasing in infant and junior schools. Secondly, most surveys indicate that teachers perceive the problem as getting worse, and whether the statistical evidence supports their views is of secondary importance because they are the people who have to face the difficult pupils. And as the W. I. Thomas dictum alerts us – if teachers perceive an increase in frequency and intensity then they will proceed to conduct themselves in accordance with that perception.

The importance of our very brief analysis is that it places the extent and nature of disruptive behaviour in perspective, for it is only when we more clearly understand the problem can we devise strategies to deal with it. In the Elton Report the kinds of behaviour primary school teachers (over 80 per cent) reported having to deal with in their classroom at least once during the week of the survey, were 'talking out of turn', 'hindering other pupils' and 'making unnecessary (non-verbal) noises'. In the course of their duties around the school, the vast majority (over 80 per cent) reported encountering pupils showing a 'lack of concern for others'. Over 60 per cent also commented on 'general rowdiness' and 'physical and verbal abuse towards other children'.

When asked about the strategies and sanctions they used, over 80 per cent of primary teachers referred to 'reasoning with pupils, both in the classroom and outside it', as well as 'class discussions about why things were going wrong'. The most commonly used sanction (71 per cent) was 'removing privileges'.

On this evidence there would seem to be little need for the introduction of severe and harsh measures. Amongst its 138 recommendations the Elton Report focuses on improved school management, improved teacher classroom management and skills. In the context of secondary schools it has much to say about pastoral care but, when one reflects on the kinds of inappropriate behaviours displayed by primary pupils, it is equally evident that there should be an emphasis on improving social skills, consideration for the needs of others and respect for people and property in primary schools too.

Alternative approaches to disruptive behaviour

The approach a school or teacher may adopt in coping with disruptive behaviour will depend to a considerable extent on whether they regard the causes of the behaviour as being outside the school's sphere of control, that is, that they are innate or the result of adverse familial or societal influences, or whether they regard the school or their own behaviour as being contributory factors. Consequently, attitudes towards indiscipline will determine whether they adopt a crisis-management, interventionist or preventative approach to problem behaviour. (For a more detailed treatment of these approaches see Tattum, 1989a,c.)

A *crisis-management approach* is reactive in its policy and locates the problem in the child. In focusing mainly on the individual child it seeks 'both cause and cure within the sphere of the pupil's individual psychology' (Frude, 1984) and is referred to as the medical model. This response has resulted in the setting up of special units or school support units (see Tattum, 1982). Other responses include exclusion from school and the range of other punishments available to teachers (see Fig. 5).

Fig. 5: Alternative approaches to disruptive behaviour

CRISIS-MANAGEMENT	INTERVENTIONIST APPROACHES	PREVENTATIVE APPROACHES
Transfer to special unit	Contracts	Pre-service training
Exclusion	Time-out room	In-service training
Punishments	On report	Whole-school discipline policy
	Letter to parent(s)	
	Support teams	
	Support agencies	

Interventionist approaches are also relative in that they too respond to problems as they arise but, at least, look beyond the child for understanding and aim to construct more beneficial relationships and structures. The intervention can involve a whole school, a classroom, group or individual child, and the objective is to initiate person and/or organisational change. As Fig. 5 shows the school/teacher may initiate the interventions or they may invite in support teams or agencies such as psychologists, local authority advisers, peripatetic support teachers and so on (Topping, 1986).

Fig. 6: Factors which contribute to a whole-school approach to discipline

A. Good teacher–pupil relations.
B. Clearly defined and understood channels of pupils' referrals.
C. Consistent application of behaviour standards to all pupils.
D. Effective classroom management techniques.
E. A developed cross-curricular PSE programme.
F. High pupil self-esteem.
G. Support by senior colleagues.
H. Good teacher communication skills – verbal and non-verbal.
I. Establishing and maintaining classroom behaviour and standards early on.
J. Emphasis placed on rewards rather than punishment.
K. Clearly defined rules – consistently applied.
L. A code of conduct democratically arrived at.
M. Good home–school and community relations.

Finally, a *preventative approach* aims to develop structures and processes which are geared to reducing problems and anticipating crises within the school itself. Such a 'whole-school approach' to discipline (Watkins and Wagner, 1987; Tattum, 1989a,b) aims to create an ethos of good order supported by a system of monitoring pupil behaviour and progress. The ethos of a school has a somewhat indefinable quality. It is something practitioners feel and observe when they first enter a school, walk down its corridors, see the children at play and sit in on their lessons. In an attempt to identify some of the factors which contribute to a good ethos we offer a list of items in Fig. 6.

Non-school attendance

Non-school attendance has been a problem in United Kingdom schools ever since compulsory schooling was introduced in the last century, although its extent has been difficult to assess. A review of the history of absenteeism over the last hundred years shows that attendance rates have not fluctuated dramatically. The ILEA was one of the few LEAs to carry out regular surveys of attendance and the result of its annual one day surveys from 1978 to 1987 show a consistent overall attendance rate for primary schools of about 92 per cent. The rates in secondary schools are lower and have shown a marginal decline from 85 per cent in the late 1970s to just over 83 per cent in 1987 (see Table 4).

Table 4. Attendance rates

	ILEA 1987[1]		HMI 1988[2]	
	Average %	Range %	Average %	Range %
Primary	91.2	77.1–98.4	91.9	82.4–98.1
	ILEA 1987[1]		HMI 1988–9[3]	
Secondary	83.3	63.6–94.3	89.5	76.9–95.0

[1] Source: ILEA Attendance Survey 1987 (9 June 1988); census taken on 13 May 1987 (both sessions).
[2] 47 schools inspected and reported on by HMI in the calendar year 1988; figures based on two sample weeks.
[3] 36 non-selective schools inspected and reported on by HMI between Easter 1988 and Easter 1989; figures based on two sample weeks.

Two other consistent features also emerge from surveys: firstly, there are significant variations in attendance rates between schools and, secondly, there is an increase in absenteeism with age. Reid (1989) found that 18 per cent of the absentees in his survey first deliberately missed school whilst in their primary schools, and 32 per cent began to miss school in the years of their transfer to secondary school. He maintains that the last two years of primary school and the first year of secondary are critical periods for the onset of absenteeism.

The majority of absences are for legitimate reasons, such as, illness. There is, however, a persistent level of unjustified absences that may take place with parental consent (condoned absence) or without it (truancy). We must also distinguish between 'school refusal', which is an emotional problem and 'truancy', which is a behavioural problem. As teachers we should also be concerned about 'internal truancy', which consists of coming to school to get your attendance mark but skipping certain lessons. HMI offer the following list for guidance but point out that they are not mutually exclusive.

● *persistent absenteeism*: missing more than half of possible attendances in any one term;
● *intermittent absenteeism*: missing days or half days in succeeding weeks, whether in a regular or irregular pattern, adding up to a considerable number of absences over a half-term or term;
● *school refusal* (a term often interchangeable with school phobia): a symptom of underlying psychological disorder, associated with anxiety, brought on, for example, by a change in circumstances such as the loss of a parent or sibling, or a change of school;
● *justified absence*: absence for a valid reason – for example, genuine illness, approved religious observances or a death in the family;
● *unjustified absence*: unauthorised absence from school, for any period, as a result of a premeditated or spontaneous action on the part of pupil, parent or both (Pack 1977); this term includes parentally condoned absence. Unjustified absence is often referred to as 'truancy';
● *internal truancy*: when a pupil who is already registered absents himself or herself for a part or the whole of the session without leaving the school premises;
● *absconding*: when a pupil leaves the school premises having been registered as present.

(HMI, 1989)

In the past explanations of non-attendance have focused on individual, home and socio-economic circumstances (Tyerman, 1968; Davie *et al.*, 1972; Reid, 1981), although, more recently, the emphasis has switched towards an interest in school-related, contributory factors (Reynolds *et al.*, 1976; Rutter *et al.*, 1979; Reid, 1985). From these school-based research programmes there is evidence of a strong correlation between low attainment and poor attendance but a weaker one between persistent absenteeism and delinquency. In fact, schools serving similar areas show wide variations in attendance rates, which demonstrates that school policies and practices do make a difference.

The self-perpetuating phenomenon of persistent non-attendance is developed by Wilson (1989)

Failure to attend school can, of itself, set in motion a series of events, attitudes and beliefs, among staff as well as pupils, which makes a return increasingly difficult. Consequently, the original reasons for the absence can become both obscure and irrelevant. For instance, a home-based problem which sets in motion a bout of truancy may in turn create difficulties within the school, as well as further problems at home, which will have to be resolved if regular attendance is to be achieved. This is often seen in cases where parents collude with their child's absence in order to satisfy their own personal needs for company or help around the house. They then find themselves unable to get their offspring to return to school at a later date as the situation worsens or they are threatened with court action.

In the school setting the most obvious effect of prolonged absence is the failure to keep pace with and understand the academic curriculum. An initial disaffection from, and lack of interest in, the education process is thus reinforced. A low ability pupil with a poor record of attendance may eventually find himself unsuitable for mainstream education. Moreover, failure to attend school can also result in deteriorating relationships with teaching staff which, on top of the other difficulties, can make the initial problem considerably worse... The typical, unfavourable reception which absentees receive when returning to school after a long absence often acts as a considerable disincentive to taking the plunge and returning the next time.

(Wilson, 1989)

Concern about an escalating pattern of absenteeism throughout a pupil's career reinforces the importance of early identification and preventative measures. As we have read, failure to keep pace with academic work is a most obvious effect of prolonged absence. An initial disaffection is reinforced and alienation can result. Other difficulties may be deteriorating relationships with teacher and helping agencies, such as, Educational Welfare Officers (EWO) and Social Workers.

From his extensive research in the problem Reid lists the following reasons for persistent absenteeism:

(a) boredom in lessons as a result of inactivity;
(b) falling behind in school work and not being 'assisted' to catch up;
(c) an unsuitable curriculum;
(d) perceived bullying, extortion, or internal classroom strife;
(e) alleged teacher–pupil conflicts;
(f) inadequate pastoral care/counselling;

(g) feelings that school was a less rewarding place for them than their more able peers; and

(h) being unable to comply with school rules and regulations (especially relating to books, materials, games kit and school uniform).

(Reid, 1985)

A starting point for our concern about the personal and social development of children is contained in Reid's contention that

> most truants tend to be shy, inward-looking and grateful for any interest or help we may offer them. They have experienced failure but long for success. But their opportunities to achieve school success are limited as they come from low income families and usually do not have the intellectual capacity to succeed with academic tasks in school.

(Reid, 1985)

All of which suggests that teachers have an important part to play in combatting truancy rates in schools, and the most recent government pronouncement, as part of its Citizens' Charter (for parents), is that schools must annually present their attendance figures to parents.

In order to improve and maintain attendance rates there must be scrupulous marking of registers, careful monitoring of the attendance of individual pupils and a prompt follow-up action where required. Notes explaining reason for absence must be insisted on, collected and checked. When truancy is suspected, parents should be notified as quickly as possible, and EWO's informed – they also have an important social and welfare role with cases of condoned absenteeism. But, as with our analysis of disruptive behaviour these are in the crisis-management and interventionist modes. What is required is a positive, preventative approach which recognises that the quality of a school's ethos and its curriculum are important factors in making children want to attend school. Similarly, schools should develop strategies for receiving back frequent absentees, aimed at helping them to catch up with missed work and making them feel welcomed and wanted.

In their report on *Attendance at Schools* HMI give a comprehensive list of strategies to promote and reward good attendance. The importance of praise and rewards are discussed in greater detail in the following chapter on teacher expectation.

● sending letters to parents of new pupils after the first possible 100 attendances with special praise both for those with 100% attendance and for those with no avoidable absences;

awarding certificates for punctuality and attendance;

holding inter-class or inter-house competitions for the best or most markedly improved attendance;

recording attendance on reports sent home, with positive comments for effort;

entering improvements on the school record of a poor attender;

sending children to senior members of staff for commendation of efforts made towards improvement as well as for full attendance;

setting up a sub-committee of school governors to meet with poor attenders and encourage them to return at a later date to talk about improvements they had made;

identifying children 'at risk' before they transfer to another class or group or school and devising ways of supporting them;

including attendance-related matters in the induction programme for all new staff and in particular for newly qualified teachers;

devising flexible and innovative responses to those who find it difficult to attend regularly for whatever reason;

setting attainment goals for individuals or class or year groups;

welcoming children back after illness;

● taking specific measures to ease children back into school after protracted absence;

● briefing teachers on how to organise the work of a class to allow for returning absentees without loss of momentum for the class as a whole.

(HMI, 1989)

Exercises

(1) Consider how the continuities–discontinuities of status can operate in a school.

(2) Discuss the process of entry into pupilhood as parents hand over the young child to the class teacher/headteacher – and the 'Does he take sugar?' syndrome, of talking about the child as if he was not present, operates.

(3) Consider professional socialisation as a process of status passage – from behind the desk to in front of the class. Also, discuss whether we should completely dispense with teacher training courses and place all training in the hands of schools.

(4) Either place the list of items in Fig. 6 in your personal order of priority or, as a class, each choose their top three items and see what are the class' priorities. These should provide ample discussion about the relationships between individual items and the complexity of a whole-school approach.

(5) Have you any further strategies to add to the HMI list of ways to promote and reward good attendance (p. 73)?

Additional reading

1. Tattum, D. P. (1989a) pp. 64–82, has a detailed discussion of Alternative Approaches to Disruptive Behaviour.
2. For a comprehensive review of how schools should cope with persistent absenteeism see Reid (1989), pp. 116–30.
3. For a wider discussion of pupil coping strategies see Woods, P. (1980) (ed.) *Pupil Strategies. Explorations in the Sociology of the School.* Croom Helm, London.

PART TWO

The Social Context of the Primary School

Introduction

The model of socialisation presented in Part 1 was that in which each individual is actively involved in his own learning. The approach argues that social interaction is fundamental to the development of 'self', though the self does not only interact with 'others' but with the meanings each person attaches to the physical environment. In the next three chapters we shall examine the personal and social development of children in the social context of the primary school. The social context is divided into three interrelated and interdependent components – they are sub-divided for purposes of space and convenience. The three components are the administrative, organis-

Fig. 7: The social context

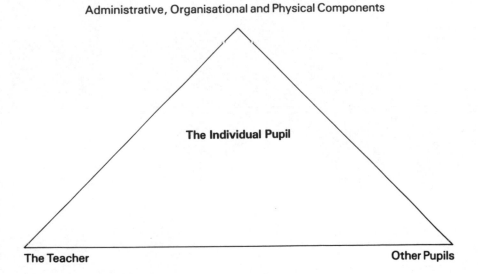

Administrative, Organisational and Physical Components

The Individual Pupil

The Teacher   Other Pupils

ational and physical aspects of schools; the teacher as the most significant other; and pupils as both significant others and collectively as an influential reference group.

The social context as conceived of in Fig. 7 creates the cognitive, emotional and social climate in which the child will learn about self and others. It is the hot-bed of social education and personal development of primary schooling.

In books which deal with the social context of teaching–learning it is usual practice to start with a discussion of the teacher's role as the most important single person, and then to progress to other aspects of the context. In this book we intend starting with an examination of the administrative and physical features, mainly because they provide the setting in which both teacher and pupils must operate. What kind of impression does a new teacher or new pupil have of the school as they enter it on their first day? What are the constraints placed upon both parties by the existent administrative and physical demands of the school? Are there structural features which will strongly influence the nature of the interaction which will take place in school and classroom? These and other factors influence teacher expectations and demands, and pupil performance and behaviour; and that is why we have chosen to look at the hidden curriculum; rules, routines and rituals; rewards and punishments; and the grouping of pupils. For the pre-existent school shapes the *definition of the situation* in which both parties must get to know each other and the social context in which they will be gradually socialised into the school's ways.

CHAPTER 4

The Administrative, Organisational and Physical Components of Social Education

In the previous three chapters we examined the concept of socialisation but, most particularly, within a symbolic interactionist approach. An approach which focuses on the development of self within an active framework, as the individual constantly reflects, not only on the behaviour of others, but on his own behaviour and its impact on others. We then looked at the part played by the family in this ongoing process of socialisation and then, in Chapter 3, concentrated on the transition of the child from home to school and into pupilhood. Throughout Symbolic Interactionism the individual child is regarded as entering into interactions and negotiations in all kinds of social settings. There is a danger with this presentation that the child is viewed as having the freedom to do just as he wishes but, as we are aware, in all social contexts there are those who have the power to insist that we conform to their demands – this exists in the differential power relations between teachers and pupils (Tattum, 1982). But institutions also impose constraints on all members' behaviour, whether it be a family or church, factory or office, military establishment or prison, or, as in our case, a school. Therefore, in order to function – even survive, we must learn the procedures, demands, expectations and relational networks of each institution we enter. Thus, a child needs to learn to give meaning to those special features which make a school – corridors, toilets, staffroom, secretary's office, dining hall, the playground and so on. Into this concept of *space* the child has to function in highly specialised *time* sequences. Very young ones will ask at morning playtime, 'Is it time to go home?', 'Do we go for dinner now?'

Each cohort will enter an objective social structure and network of existing relationships, and will engage in learning the shared meanings through interaction with other older children. But it would be wrong to believe that a consensus is produced or could exist in a differentiated community such as a school. Whilst the teacher will work towards an official definition of the situation, some pupils, as we saw in the previous chapter, will seek to redefine that situation to their own best advantage, as they perceive it. Some will like school whilst others will hate it; some will enjoy maths but others will prefer games; some will like their teacher others will not; and there will be those who look forward to playtimes and some who will not. These attitudes, values and perceptions will be learned over time through interpersonal interaction. In an attempt to summarise the social perspective which we have been exploring Meltzer *et al.* (1975) refer to three basic premises.

(1) Human beings act towards things on the basis of the meanings that the things have for them;

(2) these meanings are a product of social interaction in human society;

(3) these meanings are modified and handled through an interpretive process that is used by each person in dialogue with the things he/she encounters.

What meanings does a school have for children? Are there differing perceptions according to age, sex and social origins? To fit into the school a child must cope with a vast amount of social learning and the hidden curriculum is a very important part of that process.

The hidden curriculum

There has never been a time when the school curriculum has received so much intense attention. The nation's progress to a curriculum for all has produced a mountain of documents and been the topic of meetings ranging from Cabinet briefings to parent–teacher evenings. But the National Curriculum is more particularly concerned with the product of learning than the process, that is, the content of lessons, knowledge that must be acquired, and even testing to see if children know the facts. But what we are concerned with here are those things which make the delivery of the formal curriculum possible. In addition to being an intellectual activity, schooling is also a social experience, and it could be argued that before a child can effectively cope with the formal or official curriculum he must first come to terms with the hidden curriculum. The hidden curriculum has been variously described as those things to do with schooling which do not fit into the 'formal' or 'official' curriculum. But that is too simple, as the two are intertwined such that they are difficult to separate. To illustrate we could very briefly consider rules, which are both formally written in handbooks but informally pervade the whole school. Furthermore, to call it the 'hidden' curriculum is misleading as much of it is abundantly obvious to those who seek to understand what goes on in schools. The aspects we shall examine are part of the 'taken for granted' features of every school, which new members must learn as they negotiate a minimum of eleven years of compulsory schooling.

The concept is clearly complex, even ambiguous, and for that reason many writers on the curriculum have chosen to ignore the hidden curriculum. One writer who has attempted to tackle it in all its intricacies is Meighan (1986) and he devotes eight chapters to such elements as space, time, organisation, language, testing and marking. But it is to Jackson (1968) we must turn for the earliest, insightful analysis in his book *Life in Classrooms*. Here he argues that schooling is a preparation for life but not in the sense in which it is frequently used. For he discusses the undercurrent of experiences that have been organised to produce a level of conformity which is the normal condition of living and working together. He thus stresses three aspects of the hidden curriculum which may be introduced by the key words: *crowds, praise* and *power*.

The first fact is that life in a classroom is life in a crowd. Most of the things that are done in classrooms are done with others, or at least in their presence, and this has profound implications for the personal and social learning of a child. In this crowd the child experiences delay, denial, interruptions and distraction. A classroom is a busy place in which the teacher has the problem of organising the demands of about 30 pupils.

One of the inevitable outcomes of this complicated traffic management is the experiencing of *delay*. Children are forced to take turns for access to limited resources, including teacher's attention. If one were to 'shadow' a pupil for a day we are sure we would be surprised by the time spent waiting.

Denial occurs when permission is refused, a raised hand is ignored or the teacher insists on everyone working silently in their correct seat. *Interruptions* of many sorts create a third feature of classroom life that results, in part, from the crowded social conditions. The routine of the day will interrupt work, as will the entrance of other children bearing messages or lost property. Things happen on time in schools, for if teachers were always to wait until every pupil had completed one activity before they began another, the school day would become interminable. Linked to interruptions is the fourth element, which is, at its most basic, that every child has potentially 29 other sources of *distraction* in the room. There is an undercurrent of pupil interaction which a teacher can only partially know about. To be a successful pupil a child must learn how to be alone in a crowd, how to get on with his own work when others are fooling about.

For the child the consequence of being one in a crowd suffering frustration is to learn patience, which

> represents balance, and sometimes a precarious one, between two opposed tendencies. On the one hand is the impulse to act on desire, to blurt out the answer, to push to the front of the line, or to express anger when interrupted. On the other hand, is the impulse to give up the desire itself, to stop participating in the discussion, to go without a drink when the line is so long, or to abandon an interrupted activity.
>
> (Jackson, 1968)

The central question for the teacher is how each child sets about coping with these institutional demands, for different pupils will adopt different strategies.

The second feature of life in classrooms is that praise and reproof are delivered in public. In comparison with the private, confidential evaluation in the family, reward and punishment take place in the public glare of the rest of the class. The main source of evaluation is obviously the class teacher but a second audience also pass judgements – and they are classmates. In satisfying these two audiences a child soon realises that both academic performance and behaviour are being assessed. Regular tests are an important part of evaluation and the marks awarded are themselves sources of reward or reproof. The introduction of SATS into the curriculum attainment, and in association with national testing, is a formalised but limited form of evaluation. And as punishment and reward are such an integral part of classroom life we shall discuss them in greater detail later in this chapter (pp. 88–91). From this public evaluation pupils learn compliance and conformity, or, in some cases, the strategies necessary to satisfy teacher's expectations whilst remaining one of the crowd.

Holt (1969) describes some of the strategies that children devise to reduce the anxieties of classroom life. There is, 'right answerism', which is a collection of strategies to obtain the correct answer or an approved response. This includes reading teachers' facial clues, sequencing of questions, giving mumbled answers or, if asked, feigning confusion with, 'Oh, I forget'. Children also learn not to put their hands up too soon and instead join the forest of hands so that the chance of being called on is small.

The fact of unequal power is the third feature of classroom life to which pupils must become accustomed. The difference in authority between teacher and pupil is related to the evaluative aspect of classrooms. Primary school teachers work hard to make their classrooms warm, cheerful and friendly places – they want their children to be happy. And yet, in their relations with individual children they must exercise power. It is used to teach and enforce punctuality, attentiveness, obedience and compliance with teacher expectations. Children soon learn that there are things that they must do or they will be punished, and teacher authority grants her access to a range of punishments – some of which will physically hurt.

The associate fact in this exercise of power is that it is wielded by a relative stranger. And even though many children become quite attached to their teacher, still the dominant relationship must remain quite impersonal when compared with the intimacy of relationships in the home. Thus, children must learn to take orders from adults who do not know them very well and whom they do not themselves know intimately. Teachers of young children are often uncomfortable with this portrayal of themselves but it is in the reception and infant classes that children learn obedience and docility. Fortunately, most children accept the teacher's definition of the situation, most of the time they proceed to 'please teacher'. But this does not mean that children are passive participants in classroom interaction. For, within the class-room arena, pupils quickly learn the boundaries and constraints of behaviour and work out strategies of survival. Each pupil negotiates to maintain her/his credibility with both teacher and other pupils; ways of maximising rewards and minimising sanctions; and knowing just how far to go before testing teacher's tolerance too much. It is a matter of social learning for personal survival and the social order for each day has to be renegotiated. Classroom relations are not constants, they change with the lesson, weather, time of day, day of the week, plus many other variables.

Rules, rituals and routines

Rules, routines and ritual are the other 3Rs of schools and they too are part of the hidden curriculum. That they are integral aspects of the previous section on crowds, praise and power will be self-evident, for they are the organisational procedures a teacher will use to control the behaviour of the class and legitimise her authority.

Primary age children are lively, noisy, unpredictable and, at times, irrational in their behaviour. Wherever large numbers of people, adults or children gather there is need for rules and regulations, routines and rituals to enable the organisation to run smoothly and ensure the rights and responsibilities of all present. All social life is governed by rules with varying degrees of formality and schools are social places. It is in school that children first encounter a formal rule system. They have rules at home about mealtimes, bedtimes, watching TV and so on, but these are limited in number. Similarly, families have routines and rituals about tidying up toys, bathtimes, saying prayers before settling to sleep, etc., and these routines become ritualised behaviour which can be reassuring and comforting for the child. Children love the repetitive ritual of family games, nursery rhymes and story reading, and are quick to correct any deviation from the ritual. In this way ritual becomes habituated behaviour which serves both child and adult. We all want children to have good habits of behaviour but we cannot assume that they know the rules. Routines and rituals serve to inform and reinforce the system of rules.

In primary schools we have routines which formalise entry into school and classroom, also leaving the classroom at playtimes – in both cases the aim is to achieve a quiet and orderly entry and dismissal. Morning assembly is another good example of ritual as classes gather row by row, age by age – and sometimes, sex by sex. Children enjoy rituals and can enter into them as game play.

When visiting schools to see students on teaching practice a tutor has an excellent opportunity to observe at first hand the hidden curriculum of the 3Rs in operation in different schools. Arriving at the end of playtimes can be a revelation. On one visit to a junior school I (D. T.) entered the school yard as playtime ended. There was a single, loud blast on the deputy head's whistle and all the children stopped whatever they were doing – some froze like statues. On the second blast they all ran to take up their lines – by class and sex. The assembly area was flagged by two foot square flags and the children had to place their toes on the front edge of the flag to space out their lines. Teachers walked up and down their class lines to check that all properly positioned themselves. A signal from the deputy head and standard one girls, followed by the boys, walked smartly into school. So the ritual of entering school was performed four times a day – weather permitting. This performance will be regarded as being too formal by many teachers but for that school it served many purposes, none more important than settling down the children and making a clear distinction between playtime and lesson time. And once the children enter their own classrooms all teachers have rituals to do with greetings, giving out and collecting books, holding the door open, closing windows, putting chairs down and back on the desks at the end of the day. During each day the teacher will remind the children with, 'And what is our class rule?'.

Children are born into a world of rules and the school is the intermediary between the close, intimate family and adult society, and it is the role of the teacher to inculcate respect for the rules of social life. Schools have many rules, from formal, operational rules which regulate pupils' behaviour to more pervasively, informal, unspoken, social rules which affect every aspect of a pupil's life. As rule-governed organisations it is conceivable that every act a pupil performs is covered by some rule or other, and if no specific rule exists then a teacher will create one to cover the case as happens in this extract from *Alice in Wonderland*.

> At this moment the King, who had been for some time busily writing in his note-book, called out 'Silence!' and read out from his book, 'Rule Forty-two. All persons more than a mile high to leave the court.' Everybody looked at Alice.
>
> 'I'm not a mile high,' said Alice.
>
> 'You are,' said the King.
>
> 'Nearly two miles high,' added the Queen.
>
> 'Well, I shan't go, at any rate,' said Alice; 'beside, that's not a regular rule; you invented it just now.'
>
> 'It's the oldest rule in the book,' said the King.
>
> 'Then it ought to be Number One,' said Alice. The King turned pale, and shut his note-book hastily.
>
> (Lewis Carroll)

A more detailed consideration of the 'hidden curriculum of rules' can be found in Tattum (1982), where rules and values are linked.

> Rules give substance and expression to values; they are the symbols of beliefs and attitudes. As creators and enforcers of school rules teachers give meaning to their preferences for the particular forms of social behaviour that they deem worthwhile and desirable . . . Values, however, are vague and general, whilst rules are more specific and are intended to apply to identifiable situations. But rules are rarely so precise that they

eliminate alternative courses of action, partly because they have to be applied by people who may not agree with the underpinning values; and in a staffroom there will be a diversity of values. What is more, personally held values can be in conflict with each other so that courses of action cannot be predicted. A teacher may have trouble reconciling a belief in academic excellence and working towards equal educational opportunity.

(Tattum, 1982)

In discussions with primary school teachers about school rules, many claimed that their school had very few rules, and that the guiding principle for all was that each person should show respect for the rights of others, or some alternative expression of the Christian ethic, 'Do unto others as you would have them do unto you.' But that is a catch-all expectation which leaves pupils in a social world of uncertainty. Duke (1978) found quite the reverse, as many of the teachers he interviewed admitted to being inconsistent and justified their behaviour on the grounds that there were too many school rules for any individual to enforce effectively. In similar vein, only on a few occasions have teachers been able to say that their school had engaged in a general staff discussion of their rule system in order to devise a school-wide policy. This should change gradually as the 1988 Education Act requires all schools to draw up a School Discipline Policy Statement. Rules are the fabric of school discipline, and together with routine and ritual are the main mechanisms used to achieve and maintain good order. They are implicit in all social relationships and are explicit instruments of authority.

Despite the importance of rules few writers on education even mention them, and those who do give them only passing reference. Part of the problem is that rules are one of those 'taken for granted' features of school life which challenges categorisation. Many of those who do write about school rules do so from an interest in rule-breaking, that is, deviant behaviour. But in looking at disruptive behaviour researchers have highlighted the pervasiveness and complexity of school rules which children have to learn and negotiate around as part of normal life in school.

Teachers should be seen to be fair, neither having favourites nor picking on individuals, but there is evidence that preferential treatment is given to certain pupils because of their social or academic status (Lufler, 1979; Hollingsworth et al., 1984). Not all pupils are treated the same by teachers, for there is the human practice of rewarding those who conform most closely to the ideal pupil role as a teacher perceives it and punishing those who deviate most prominently from perceived expectations. Differential treatment based on reputation or organised labelling is amply recorded (Hargreaves, 1967; Lacey, 1970). Inconsistencies among teachers are most evident as the teachers display variable commitment to the enforcement of school rules as they move about the building. Many teachers concentrate on maintaining good discipline in their own classrooms and hold to the view that about-school discipline is the responsibility of the headteacher and other senior colleagues. Unfortunately, this differential response to good order results in different treatment for the same offence.

But a close examination of the relationship between rules and behaviour reveals that rules are not fixed and immutable, but are open to interpretation, negotiation and modification. We cannot predict which rule a teacher will apply or whether a rule will be invoked at all – she may look the other way or select from a range of alternative responses. What is more, the violator may plead innocence, ignorance of the rule, provocation or whatever, and so negotiate a modified response.

That schools are hidebound by rules has already been noted; their rules range from the legal and formal, through varying degrees of informality. At one point in their study of deviant behaviour in classrooms, Hargreaves *et al.* despairingly wrote:

> We were in danger of becoming depressed by the sheer quantity and complexity of what to us appeared to be the rules at work in the classrooms. Rarely were these rules stated in any explicit form. How then were we to make sense of the data in which we were steadily beginning to drown?
>
> (Hargreaves *et al.*, 1975)

To try to give form to the rule structure they originally classified the school rules as: institutional, situational and personal; the latter they subsequently elaborated around the themes of talk, movement, time, and teacher–pupil and pupil–pupil relationships.

In an attempt to produce a more comprehensive categorisation of a complex and ambiguous rules system, Duke (1978) devised the following list:

(1) Attendance related rules
(2) Rules related to out-of-class behaviour
    (a) Criminal conduct
    (b) Non-criminal conduct

(3)   Rules related to classroom behaviour
       (a) Classroom Deportment
       (b) Conduct related to academic work

Duke later suggested

> that many of the student behaviour problems now perplexing
> education result from inconsistencies and ineffective practices
> connected with school rules themselves. The implication is that some
> improvements in school discipline may be brought through
> organisational rather than behavioural change.
>
> (Duke, 1978)

In a further attempt to understand the complexity of school rules
Tattum (1982) has elaborated the extent and nature within a five-fold
categorisation. The categories are not intended to be discrete, as they
bring together the interaction between laws governing compulsory
attendance and interpersonal negotiations between teacher and pupil.

(1)   Legal/quasi-legal rules
(2)   Organisational rules
(3)   Contextual rules
(4)   Personal rules
(5)   Relational rules

School governance is a complex problem of which rules are only one
aspect, but there is a growing body of knowledge which indicates that
the ways in which schools organise themselves influence relationships
and levels of disaffection.

At this stage we will briefly discuss each category as it operates in
primary schools. The categories are not discrete as the higher-order
rules enter into social contexts and relationships.

(1)   *Legal or quasi-legal* regulations take us into the realm of the law
       as regular, compulsory school attendance is required. Here we
       highlight concerns about truancy and absenteeism, as well as
       skipping lessons. The regulations also extend into punctuality
       and bringing a note from home to explain an absence.
           The legal authority of headteachers with their Governing Body
       permits them to act in all areas of school life. Regulations relating
       to dress and general appearance are to be found in all maintained
       schools – matters such as the wearing of uniform and not wearing
       jewellery.

(2) *Organisational rules* are those which are necessary for the school's smooth running and good order. They control movement about the building and identify forbidden places and behaviour. Examples include no running, no litter or graffiti, or interfering with school property, such as fire alarms, hoses and other potentially dangerous equipment. Registers must be marked, monies collected and homework (where approved) given in on time. Classrooms must be evacuated at break-times; the use of cloakrooms and toilets are regulated; behaviour in the dining room and playground has many rules. There is a profusion of rules to regulate behaviour about the school building.

(3) *Contextual rules* apply mainly to behaviour in classrooms compared with the general school rules of the previous section. Different school subjects or activities make varying demands upon pupils in the three areas of conduct, task and dress. In the early years children will wear tabards when working on water activities or painting, and aprons when making cakes or cooking. Games and PE are good examples of regulations about dress and conduct, as is swimming, where rules of safety will apply.

Hargreaves *et al.* (1975) elaborated their situational rules around themes: talk, movement, time, teacher–pupil relationships and pupil–pupil relationships. Each theme contains a range of rules, some common to most teachers – such as not talking when teacher is talking, whilst others are more individualistic – such as the level of noise permissible or talking to your neighbour.

(4) *Personal rules* progress from the previous example, as they are an individual teacher's operating rules. For the pupil, survival is dependent on knowing the operating rules and 'teacher-testing' is part of the negotiating process as pupils try to work out the personal rules of each teacher. 'First encounters' is a time in any interaction when a great deal of interpretive work is done by teacher and pupils. The initiative in classroom interaction rests with the teacher and so during initial encounters the teacher must make known her boundaries of tolerance. This is most important with new teachers to the profession or school, or just new to that particular class. Pupils want to know their teacher as a person, is she interesting and so on. Several studies have demonstrated that pupils prefer teachers who are 'strict'. Strictness is associated with 'laying down the ground rules', which, from the pupil's viewpoint, means 'knowing where you stand'.

(5) Finally, *relational rules* regulate the interpersonal interactions between teacher and pupil, and pupil and pupil. Obedience, politeness and respect are the essential relational rules that teachers hold. Rules of action cover acts of defiance, refusal to cooperate, rudeness and disrespect, dishonesty, physical violence or threat of it. Rules of word would extend to answering back, giving cheek, arguing or dissenting, abuse and swearing. Teachers reduce pupil–pupil relational rules to consideration and care – no bullying, physical or verbal abuse, theft, swearing or copying.

It is evident from the above analysis that schools have an intricate system of rules. From living and working by them children learn about citizenship; are prepared for the world of work and learn about interpersonal negotiation, which is at the centre of all relationships – however brief; and their personal development expands as they learn more about themselves.

Punishments and rewards

Discussion of rules leads naturally into punishing those who break them and rewarding children who abide by them. We shall be very brief in our treatment of punishment as we wish to take a more positive approach to the personal and social education of a child by concentrating on praise, incentives and rewards. As a profession teaching has spent much more time and effort devising ways of punishing children than it has in working on a system of rewards. In fact, the literature on rewards is very limited.

Whenever a pupil breaks a rule the range of reactions open to a teacher is considerable. If a pupil misbehaves a teacher may:

(1) ignore the act – probably the most frequent reaction;
(2) indicate disapproval by look or gesture;
(3) give a verbal reprimand – in private or in public;
(4) withhold privileges;
(5) give lines, stay in at playtime or some other officially approved form of punishment;
(6) send the pupil to stand outside the classroom:
(7) use unofficial physical punishment;
(8) send the pupil to the head or another senior member of staff;
(9) send for the parents;

(10) ultimately refuse to teach the pupil or demand severe measures to be taken, such as exclusion, the involvement of other agencies, transfer to a special unit.

The list is not exhaustive but it does indicate the range of teacher reactions, about which there will be uncertainty over detection and the severity of the teacher's response. Many pupils (Tattum, 1982) are critical of the inconsistent way teachers treat different children for the same misbehaviour. Many teachers may well say that differential treatment is not only inevitable but desirable, as they seek to fit the punishment to the child and their knowledge of him. A mere look may be all that is needed to quieten the noisy behaviour of one child but another may need a harsh reprimand or be made to sit next to teacher. From the perception of the pupils though these inconsistencies can appear unfair and unjust.

Punishment and rewards go hand-in-hand in schools as they support the rule system. Together they are means of defining acceptable behaviour for children; they underline what is right and wrong. That is, they emphasise the meanings of certain actions. Talking in class is wrong and punishment makes it clear. Effort and good work are publicly rewarded. The triumph of the reception class teacher is the rapid transition of a disorganised group of rising fives into a class that behaves in a way that teacher has defined. Rewards and punishment are part of that process of socialisation but used with a very light touch by the teacher.

In a crowded classroom teacher cannot arrange for all to succeed, although the lack of rewards for large numbers of children remains a weakness of teaching. There is a tendency for teachers (and schools) to concentrate their efforts on the few who are rewarding to teacher. They, in turn, receive the attention, praise and prizes. But at the back of every primary class will be some pupils who will spend ten years of schooling without much achievement or rewards.

Withey (1979) classifies rewards into four categories:

(1) Material rewards – prizes, trophies and badges.
(2) Symbolic rewards – title, status or housepoints.
(3) Assessment – marks, grades, stars and similar devices.
(4) Teacher reactions – as in praise, encouragement, approval and recognition.

When considering the functions of a reward, these may be varied and interrelated. For example, a reward may serve to promote the institutional aims of the school, to provide a mechanism for competition (as in a house system), to provide an incentive and also a reinforcement of approved behaviour, and in the area of formal qualifications, rewards officially confirm a pupil's achievement. A rewards system would therefore appear to have several functions for a school but it also serves the interest of pupils, and it is this dynamic interaction that needs to be considered. The effectiveness of a rewards system is therefore highly dependent on the way in which it is regarded by the pupils as well as the staff. A number of studies in secondary schools reveal a high degree of consistency in their findings of pupils' perceptions of the relative merits of various rewards and punishments, which do not always coincide with the perceptions of teachers.

The range of rewards and incentives available to schools is extensive. Before considering the types of rewards favoured by pupils, we offer the National Association of Head Teachers (1984) comprehensive list for consideration. It does not claim to be exhaustive, neither are the rewards placed in a precise value order. The many-sidedness of praise and rewards means that they can be delivered in formal or informal ways, in public or in private, to individuals or groups, and they can be incremental or given for a particularly worthy achievement.

The rewards given in the NAHT list include:

- a quiet word or a pat on the back;
- an exercise book comment, either in general terms – 'well done', or in a more detailed way, picking out specific points or ideas that gave pleasure;
- a visit to a more senior member of staff and/or the headteacher for commendation, for example a written comment, star, etc;
- a public word of praise in front of a group, a class, a year or the whole school;
- public written acknowledgement through a special Merit Record Book of some kind;
- public acknowledgement by presentation at an assembly or by giving some special responsibility;
- some system of merit marks or points, with or without public acknowledgement of that award;
- marks, grades and assessments – for behaviour as well as work – but having some danger of an adverse effect on those excluded;
- school badges or certificates, formally presented or otherwise, for good behaviour, community support or positive attitude;

- prizes which reflect attitudes, not least of service in the community;
- use of school reports to comment favourably, not only on good work and academic achievement, but on behaviour, on involvement and on general attitudes;
- a letter to parents informing them specifically of some action or achievement deserving praise. (Too often schools write only when something has gone wrong.)

The range of rewards is extensive but many of them are symbolic, that is, they are built into the culture of the school. This means that children have to identify with the school culture and learn to value marks, good reports and public praise. Once learned these rewards are capable of motivating children to enter the role of pupil with all the benefits that contains for self and school. The importance of rewards in this process cannot be over-emphasised. Children must experience praise and rewards too before they can value them. This is most important with very young children because of their emotional attachment to the class teacher. Young children are keen for teacher's attention and eager to know that teacher likes them. In this context rewards are inducements in the personal and social development of children, and this aspect of self-esteem will figure predominantly in the following two chapters – both teacher and other pupils dispense rewards and praise.

Surprisingly, very little research has been carried out in the area of rewards except, that is, by people who advocate the use of behaviour modification techniques. But that approach conflicts with the whole thesis of this work, as we have emphasised the individual's capacity to reflect on his own behaviour as well as that of others. Furthermore, the controlled environment of behaviourist theory does not take into account the complexity of subtle interaction engaged in between teacher and pupil or pupil and pupil. It is the conscious interpretation of other interactions that gives them meaning.

Working 'together' in groups

Group work is another of the 'taken-for-granted' features of primary schools. In the majority of classrooms children sit around desks or tables doing their work. In fact, it is rare for one to find a class where pupils sit in seriated order working at individual or whole-class set assignments. Since the Plowden Report (1967), working in small groups has become the accepted organisational format in primary schools and, therefore, one might argue that there is nothing particularly new to learn from a section on group work. Group work existed pre-Plowden, collaborative group work was already widely adopted in the primary schools of the 1960s. Throughout the report the emphasis was on the value of individual work and groups were presented as the best balance in achieving both individualised learning and overcoming the limited number of teacher–pupil contacts in a typical sized classroom. The report also claimed social benefits, such as, learning to cooperate with one another, helping one another and the realisation of one's own and others' strengths and weaknesses.

However, subsequent research continues to confirm that whilst working in groups is commonly practised in primary schools, pupils work mainly on their own tasks. A case of sitting together but not working together. In the ORACLE Survey's report (Galton et al., 1980) over 90 per cent of the classes visited were using some form of group arrangement but when the teachers were questioned about their grouping many reported that they looked upon group work as little more than a form of seating organisation.

> In the ORACLE study it was common to see examples of joint group work in most classrooms involving common tasks but individual assignments. These joint activities, however, were seldom used for teaching basic skills of computation and English or for science, but were largely restricted to art and craft or general studies where there was a practical element. Less than a quarter of the teachers who made use of joint group work did so for more than one curriculum area.
>
> (Galton, 1990)

In a more recent investigation of curriculum provision in small schools, the PRISMS study (Galton et al., 1987) reports similar patterns of organisation in both infant and junior classrooms. The overall patterns of working showed that 79 per cent and 81 per cent of observations in infant and junior classes respectively involved a pupil working alone within a group setting. These findings are supported by studies conducted in the ILEA at infant level (Tizard et al., 1988). For the most part children sat in groups but worked individually. In other words, teachers set up social groups but prevented children from openly benefiting from the interpersonal interactions and personal development that the grouping offered.

Kerry and Sands (1982), amongst others, have argued that the principal advantage of collaborative group work is that it helps pupils to work together cooperatively and permits them to learn from each other, thus removing the stigma of failure for slow learners. Group work also improves individual pupil's self-image in that by working in groups children come to respect each other's strengths and weaknesses. For us not to openly encourage children to work 'together' when in a group is to frustrate their social inclination and deny them the positive opportunities of 'learning togetherness'.

In an early review of British and American literature in support of learning in groups Yeomans (1983) presented the following tentative conclusion. Following comments on academic achievement the following observations are made about *personal and social development*:

(1) Cooperative learning techniques have strong and consistent effects on relationships between pupils of different ethnic background.

(2) Mutual concern among pupils is increased regardless of the structure used.

(3) There is some indication that self-confidence and self-esteem are improved.

(4) Pupils in classes using cooperative learning generally report increased liking of school.

Despite the general view that children work mainly in groups in primary schools the more innovative attempts to develop collaborative and cooperative group work have been done in developing personal and social education initiatives in secondary schools. Tutorial materials were pioneered by Button (1981) and the *Active Tutorial Work* (ATW) Series (Baldwin and Wells, 1979–84), in which the aims are to help develop youngsters' social skills, life skills and interpersonal skills. But the most advanced work in the specific area of cooperative learning has been developed in America by, amongst others, Johnson and Johnson (1987) and Slavin (1986, 1990). At Johns Hopkins University Slavin has produced and researched four pupil team learning methods. The first two are general cooperative learning approaches adaptable to most subjects and age levels. They are Student Teams–Achievement Divisions (STAD) and Teams–Games–Tournament (TGT). The other two are curricula designed for use in particular subjects, namely, Maths and Reading and Composition. Here we shall concentrate on the first pair but readers interested in all approaches should consult Slavin (1990). According to Slavin three concepts are central to these team learning methods: team rewards, individual accountability and equal opportunities for success. The idea is to encourage individuals to cooperate in working and learning together. Progress is a group concern whilst personal development is equally the group's responsibility.

In STAD pupils are placed in four member learning teams that are mixed in performance level, sex and, where appropriate, ethnicity. The teacher presents a lesson, after which the pupils work within their teams to make sure that all team members have mastered the lesson. All pupils are then required to take individual quizzes on the lesson material but they must work on their own. Children's scores are compared against their own previous averages and points are awarded based on the extent to which each child has met or exceeded their own earlier performance. These points are then added to the form team scores and teams which meet certain criteria may earn some kind of class award. The cycle of activities, from teacher lesson, team collaboration, to assignment normally extends over three to five class periods. In summarising his methods Slavin writes:

> STAD has been used in every imaginable subject, from mathematics to language arts, to social studies, and has been used from age 7 to college students. It is most appropriate for teaching well-defined objectives with single right answers, such as mathematical computations and applications, language usage and mechanics, geography and map skills, and science facts and concepts.
>
> The main idea behind Student Teams–Achievement Divisions is to motivate children to encourage and help each other to master skills presented by the teacher. If pupils want their team to earn team rewards, they must help their team-mates to learn the material. They must encourage their team-mates to do their best, expressing norms that learning is important, valuable and fun. Pupils work together after the teacher's lesson. They may work in pairs and compare answers, discuss any discrepancies, and help each other with any learning problems. They may discuss approaches to solving problems, or they may quiz each other on the content they are studying. They teach their team-mates and assess their strengths and weaknesses to help them succeed on the quizzes.
>
> (Slavin, 1990)

TGT uses the same teacher presentation and team work as in STAD, but replaces the quizzes with weekly tournaments in which pupils compete with members of other teams to contribute points to their team scores. In this way TGT adds a dimension of excitement. Team mates help one another to prepare for the games by studying worksheets and explaining problems to each other; but when pupils compete against members of other teams they must do it alone, thus ensuring individual accountability.

In a summary of academic and cognitive benefits Slavin makes the following claims:

> Co-operative learning almost never has negative effects on achievement, so teachers can reap the 'social benefits' of co-operation by simply allowing pupils to work together or by giving them problems to solve as a group. However, if they wish to use co-operative methods to accelerate pupil achievement, the research evidence is clear that they must set up co-operative activity so that their groups are rewarded (for example, with certificates, recognition, a small part of their grades) based on the individual achievement of every group member. Usually this means that pupils study together in their groups and then have their scores on individual quizzes averaged to form a team score.
>
> Do co-operative learning methods work equally well for all types of children? In general, the answer is yes. While occasional studies find particular advantages for high or low achievers, boys or girls, and so on, the great majority find equal benefits for all types of children. Sometimes a concern is expressed that co-operative learning will hold back high achievers. The research provides absolutely no support for this claim; high achievers gain from co-operative learning (relative to high achievers in traditional classes) just as much as do low and average achievers.
>
> (Slavin, 1990)

In the area of personal and social benefits children consistently express greater liking for their classmates in general as a result of participating in cooperative learning methods (Slavin, 1983), which also extends to positive inter-ethnic relations (Slavin, 1985). Both outcomes are of the kind teachers would wish to generate in all our schools. In addition, cooperative learning has been found to have the positive effect of raising children's self-esteem (Slavin, 1983), which will be developed in the next chapter as an important outcome of social relationships.

Work on cooperative learning in the UK also indicates positive outcomes. Cowie (1987) interviewed 84 secondary school teachers. Those who favoured cooperative group work referred to its benefits as being enjoyable, widening friendship groups, breaking down gender barriers, developing concepts and helping pupils become more articulate. The group work methods used included role play, discussion, team building, work relating to real tasks and problem solving. Other social and personal qualities which they felt had developed were skills of communication, learning and understanding; developing as a person; plus skills of cooperation. The benefits included in this final point are developed by Galton who writes that

> in addition to leadership roles such as identifying goals, allocating work and summarizing viewpoints, children were identified as willing followers who sometimes carried out tedious tasks such as tidying up and generally keeping things going by acting as gatekeepers. Other pupils helped resolve disputes, and attempted to bring the discussion back to the point. These teachers defined effective group work as the capacity for every child, at one time or another to act out all these roles.
>
> (Galton, 1990)

In primary schools Stoate and Thacker (1988) have been active in developing the collaborative group work advocated by Galton in combination with the personal and social objectives of the secondary schools tutorial work referred to earlier. In their training programmes Stoate and Thacker emphasise the importance of both teachers and pupils being effectively taught the methods and skills of working cooperatively in groups. These can be summarised thus:

(1) that members of supportive groups should engage in mutual help and concern;
(2) that individual people, with the support of their peers, should be at the centre of their own development;
(3) that the work should be inspired by caring, concern and a responsibility in relationships;
(4) that the work should be developmental in the sense that there will be some kind of deliberate and sequential structure that enables individuals and groups to chart their own personal exploration and development, and be helped to move along by self-conscious and manageable steps.

In their work with primary age children Stoate and Thacker (1988) are convinced of the gains in the area of PSE.

> Unlike adolescents, for whom peer group is a strong influence, seven and eight year olds are still largely influenced by the family and peer groups are only just becoming well defined and reasonably stable. However, our overall conclusions after three years are that the small support groups have a real part to play in providing an area for younger children to receive and give support and to reflect on, learn and practise personal and social skills. Group formation needs to be carefully

considered, with the children themselves involved in the decision making and with a conscious effort to encourage mixed sex grouping.
(Stoate and Thacker, 1988)

Taking up the concern about how well young children will be able to work cooperatively other writers register criticisms. For example, Bennett (1985) and Good and Brophy (1984) argue that the method 'may be less relevant and more difficult to implement for teachers working with primary grade students'. Peterson *et al.* (1985) more strongly hold to the view that children as young as seven or eight are unlikely to possess the social and cognitive skills necessary to work effectively in small groups. Others have expressed concern about the evaluation of these group methods and so it is recognised that whilst cooperative group methods offer many benefits there is a need for more systematic and rigorous research.

We need both qualitative research projects to observe the nature and quality of interactions as well as quantitative evaluation of the frequency and direction of interactive communications.

In conclusion, we believe that at this stage it would be inappropriate to present cooperative group learning methods as the panacea to classroom work. Classrooms require a 'mixed economy' of learning approaches to cater for the needs of different children and the requirements of different skills and tasks. Furthermore, we cannot expect children to cooperate simply by placing them in work groups. There is need to give them the social and interpersonal skills to enable them to personally appreciate the benefits of cooperation and to counter-balance the strong competitive ethos that runs through the whole education system.

The most positive outcome from giving pupils at least a weekly experience of cooperative group work is that it includes the essential personal and social ingredients as integral parts of a whole-curriculum process. As we look to produce a PSE curriculum for the primary school (see NCC, 1989) and work through cross-curricular themes like *Education for Citizenship* (NCC, 1990), we would do well to recall that we each learn about ourselves, as well as the social world, from interaction with others. Thus, the organisation of children's learning into cooperative groups will supplement other social and personal developmental work implicated in documents to do with cross-curricular themes. It will provide an opportunity not only for cooperation to be experienced but will give teachers the opportunities to focus, through discussion and projects, on qualities such as friendship, trust, support and sharing.

Exercises

(1) With your class discuss rules and draw up a Class Code of Behaviour.
(2) Draw a Wall Diary of birthdays, festivals and school events as a part of a project on school rituals and routines.
(3) Discuss with fellow students or colleagues how you would devise a rewards system for a whole school.
(4) Discuss the claim that most group work is not genuine cooperation and examine the *social* benefits of cooperative learning.

Additional reading

1. For a critical assessment of PSE through cooperative group work in the primary school read D. Harwood, Chapter 23, in *Thinking About – personal and social education in the primary school*, edited by Peter Lang.
2. For a brief and accessible summary of Robert Slavin's methods of cooperative learning see his Chapter 13 in *The Social Psychology of the Primary School*, edited by Colin Rogers and Peter Kutnick.

CHAPTER 5

Teacher Expectations and Pupil Concept of Self

A pupil's developing concept of self

As we have noted on a number of occasions, one of the major assumptions of the interactionist approach is that human beings invest things with meaning and thereby convert them into social objects. One of the things we invest with meaning is ourselves. We become objects to ourselves. Just as I hold opinions about other people and physical objects, I have beliefs about myself. In the opening chapter we wrote that our starting point is an understanding of the emergence of self – our progress to becoming a social person (p. 12). We thus engaged those fundamental human questions of 'Who am I?' 'What kind of person am I?' and 'Why am I me?'. In subsequent chapters we proceeded to answer these questions but here we shall discuss the most central tenet, that is, the development of the individual self-concept. For it is society which gives shape and meaning to our self-conceptualisation; and this whole idea is contained within the reflexive self. This concept, we noted, is the human quality of being able to observe and criticise our own thoughts and behaviour. It is an inner-view of self. Rosenberg (1979) defined the self-concept as 'the totality of the individual's thoughts and feelings with reference to himself as an object'. On the importance of the self-concept Burns writes:

> The self-concept . . . is becoming a most important construct in the explanation of human behaviour. The self-concept is the set of attitudes a person holds towards himself. It is an important concept because, of all the reasons for the current surge of interest in the study of human behaviour, none is more compelling than the desire of individuals to know more about themselves, to understand what makes them tick. It influences all aspects of behaviour, because the way we feel about and evaluate aspects of ourselves influences how we will function in any situation.
>
> (Burns, 1986)

99

The self-concept is learned and develops out of the mass of interpersonal interactions which bombard the individual from infancy. At first, infants cannot differentiate between themselves and the external world but gradually self-awareness develops and at the same time the child is able to view others as separate entities. As Piaget (1952) emphasised, a major achievement of the sensori-motor stage is the infant's gradual distinction between the world around them and their own self as an entity. Through motor activities the infant grasps at objects, throws them away, tinkles the suspended mobile, and so gets a sense of the world which is not himself. This kind of play serves an important role in defining the boundaries of the body, a vital stage in differentiating self from the surrounding environment.

> The self-concept, however rudimentary and diffuse, is born at the moment when the differentiation becomes a reality . . . But the process is accelerated by the advent of language – at two years old the pronouns 'mine', 'me', 'you', and 'I' come into use; such pronouns serve as conceptualizations of self and others.
>
> (Burns, 1986)

The development of self-concept proceeds from a concrete view of self to a more abstract one. Young children define themselves in terms of their appearance, name and address, possessions, friends, etc. Many of us will recall writing our name and address in the front of a book, proceeding through to Europe, Western Hemisphere, World and The Universe. Gradually children acquire a more abstract self-view and school is an important stage in this development. They develop separate awareness of different personal traits and abilities and realise that what you achieve does not always match capabilities. At school the self-concept becomes better organised and more complexed.

The process whereby we develop a definition of self is both complexed and life-long, for the self-concept is dynamic and not static. Heiss (1981) suggests that the self-concept has four 'context areas' – an identity set, a set of qualities, a set of evaluations and a set of self-confidence levels.

The *identity set* consists of positional labels which refer to the social categories to which we feel we belong. When you think of yourself as a student or a teacher, you are representing to yourself a view of whether you fit in the social world.

When we attempt to define ourselves we also refer to our *qualities* – tall, fair, conscientious, friendly, artistic and so on.

The self-concept also includes a set of *self-evaluations* which are attached to our identities and qualities. These elements of the evaluative self constitute our view of how good we are at what we are, for example, good student or poor musician.

The fourth aspect of the self-conception is the person's *levels of self-confidence*. They refer to the person's estimate of the extent to which he or she can master challenges and surmount problems, that is, the extent to which things can be made to turn out as you want them to. 'Self-confidence may be considered a function of self-evaluation measured against one's view of what is needed to control one's world' (Heiss, 1981).

The question arises whether these assertions we make about ourselves are true. And although we do not have direct access to another person's thoughts the matter can be investigated given humans' ability to talk and their self-awareness. Unlike other animals, humans can report on the contents of their thoughts. A well-known test of the self-concept is the 'Twenty-Statements' or 'Who-Am-I' test. In this test the subject is instructed: 'Ask yourself the question, "Who am I?" and answer it as if you were giving the answers to yourself, not to anyone else (see p. 102).

In simpler terms self-concept can be divided into *self-image*, that is, the totality of the wide range of ways in which each person perceives of himself and, *self-esteem*, which is the evaluation or judgement a person places on each element. Heiss' first two content areas would equate to self-image and the evaluative and self-confidence areas to self-esteem. Webster and Sobieszek (1974) make a clear distinction between *developmental* and *social* self. The *developmental* self they take as 'roughly equivalent to the set of personal characteristic, or the "personality", of the individual'. Of importance here is the notion of biological growth, and the self-concept is really viewed as the outcome of maturation. Central to the *social* self-concept is the significance of the environment in the development of personality.

From this standpoint, the personality is formed *in toto* through the sum of experiences an individual has in social relationships. This particular way of looking at personality found prominence in the writing of earlier interactionists such as Charles Horton Cooley. Writing at the turn of the century, his theory of self stresses that a person's self-concept depends very much on how the individual interprets the reactions and opinions of significant others in particular. This concept he called the '*looking-glass self*', a notion we shall return to later in greater detail.

THE SELF-IMAGE – THE TWENTY-STATEMENTS TEST

In the space below, give twenty answers to the question, 'Who am I?'

1 _____
2 _____
3 _____
4 _____
5 _____
6 _____
7 _____
8 _____
9 _____
10 _____
11 _____
12 _____
13 _____
14 _____
15 _____
16 _____
17 _____
18 _____
19 _____
20 _____

Returning to the evaluative part of the self-concept, it is accepted that there will be both positive and negative elements which are learned from our associations with other people in a variety of settings. Thus we regard the self-concept not as a singular entity but multi-dimensional and associated with the multiple roles we each play in our lives. For example, in a day a child will play the role of boy/girl, son/daughter, friend, pupil, member of a school team, and may hold separate and different self-concepts in each case.

This evaluative loading of the self-concept is learned and, since it is learned, it can alter in direction and weighting as other learning experiences are encountered . . . So self-evaluation is not fixed, it relates to each particular context.

(Burns, 1986)

We have an illustration in Lacey (1970), where he describes how some boys who had been 'best pupils' in their primary schools had to re-evaluate their academic self-definition as they were placed in low streams upon transfer to the grammar school. In comparison with brighter peers they were no longer able to sustain a self-concept which placed them at the top of the school. Similarly, each of us derives evaluative benchmarks from the surrounding environment and the feedback we receive from social relationships. The child at school will have a number of sources which contribute to his self-image and self-esteem, and Fig. 8 illustrates some of these sources.

Fig. 8: Multiple sources of self-image and self-esteem

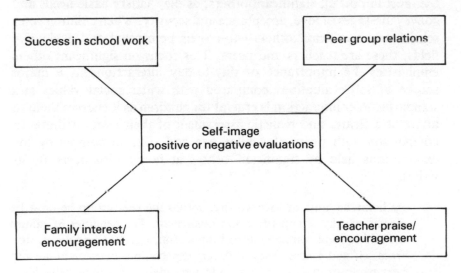

The knowledge that children acquire about themselves occurs primarily through social relationships. At school they receive many opportunities to evaluate their abilities and skills, and a major perspective of the self-concept is the 'other self', or how you think other people think of you. This subjective, interpretive feedback from others is called the *looking-glass self* (Cooley, 1902) and is a major determinant of the self-concept.

Each to each a looking-glass
Reflects the other that doth pass.

As we see our face, figure, and dress in the glass, and are interested in them because they are ours, and pleased or otherwise with them according as they do or do not answer to what we should like them to be; so in imagination we perceived in one another's mind some thought of our appearance, manners, aims, deeds, character, friends, and so on, and are variously affected by it.

(Cooley, 1902)

Our self-concepts are formed on what we think others' reactions are to us. In our daily interactions we constantly read and interpret the messages we believe other people are sending us. They may be verbal or non-verbal, such as, gestures, facial expressions, body language, which we interpret (or misinterpret) as we seek to learn what others think about us and, hence, 'What kind of person we are'.

The most influential feedback we receive comes from significant others. With infants and young children parents are presumed to be the most important significant others, as they satisfy basic needs and convey messages of love, acceptance and security. When children enter school new significant others enter their perceptual and evaluative fields, these are teachers and peers. This focus on significant others emphasises the importance of day-to-day interactions as a major source of self-evaluation, compared with wider social values and standards. Peer interaction is crucial for children as it enables them to arrive at a clearer and realistic assessment of their own attributes in comparison with peers of similar age and size. In comparing the expectations held by significant others at home with peers Burns writes:

At home he must be love-worthy, within the peer group he must be respect-worthy, competitive and competent. The penalties of failure are self-concept components of humiliation, rejection and derogation from self and others. These different expectations between home and peer group are due to the former placing a high premium on behaviour, while the latter places it on performance. In fact, behaviour unacceptable by parents may well be ignored in the peer group, or even acceptable!

(Burns, 1986)

Before leaving this section on peer influences we could profitably consider physical attributes and body image, firstly, because each person's concept of self as a physical entity is something we have to adjust to throughout life and, secondly, body image links closely with the section on bullying in the next chapter.

> After initial sex-typing by parents at birth, body size and shape is the most conspicuous physical attribute during childhood . . . A person's height, weight, complexion, eyesight and body proportions become closely associated with his attitudes to himself and feelings of personal adequacy and acceptability. Like all other elements of self-conception, the body image is subjective, but no other element is more open to private and public evaluation. The body is the most visible and sensed part of a person. We see, feel and hear a lot of ourselves; the body is a central feature in much of our self-perception.
>
> (Burns, 1986)

Social images of the ideal type of male and female bombard us from the media and other cultural communications. The messages conveyed are that males should be broad-shouldered, muscular and athletic and that well-proportioned females are likely to gain social approval. And just as children are influenced by gender stereotyping so too are they by the names other children may call them. Nicknames can be cruel and hurtful, as they often exaggerate physical characteristics. In the playground certain pupils are powerful and manipulate others to verbally tease and abuse more vulnerable children. The power of a nickname is that, as with other personal labelling, it can be generalised to describe the whole person. A boy who is called Fatso may also be seen to be lazy, poor at games, greedy, weak-willed, poor at his work and so on. Teachers should be very wary about using negative nicknames, even in a light-hearted manner, for it does give it adult approval. But nicknames can also be positive and used to raise a pupil's self-esteem, as the following true story about 'Zack the Whack' illustrates.

Zack the Whack

> Zachary is a tall, thin, gangly eight-year-old, freckle-faced with bright red hair, large hands and feet and poor coordination. He is very serious, needs constant help with his work and confidence-building. During lessons he attempts to answer questions by putting his hand up only to forget what he was going to say, and is usually supported by Matthew his bosom pal from nursery schooldays who tells us what he thinks Zachary wants to say.
>
> For games lessons Zachary is immaculately turned out in white T-shirt and red shorts (he told me he is a Liverpool supporter and hopes

to get a red shirt for his birthday). On attempting to kick the ball he falls over several times, much to the delight of some of the team. Zachary enjoys this attention and repeats his performance whenever the opportunity arises. Rounders is a popular lesson, the class organise themselves into House teams combining two Houses which are changed over at the next lesson. Several players manage to make it to first base and others even second base. Zachary puts up the bat and connects, with one almighty swing he slams the ball down the field, with a startled look on his face he is urged to run – yet another rounder is made by him. I said, 'I shall call you Zack the Whack', the children applaud. His title is repeated around the school. Now there's a smile on his face.

Fig. 9: Pupil self-concept: the academic domain

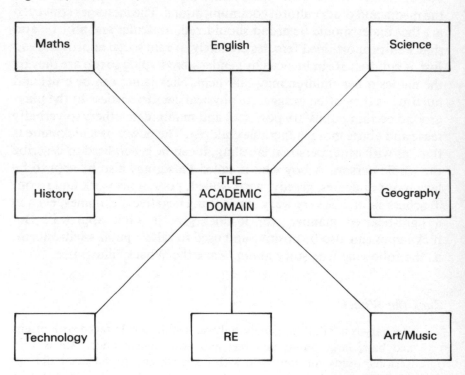

Recent research on the self-concept offers thinking that is particularly apposite to teacher–pupil relationships. The first observation is that it is hierarchically organised (Marsh and Shavelson, 1985) and, secondly, that we possess domain-specific self-perceptions. On the hierarchical ordering of the self-concept, it is argued that a

Fig. 10: Bledsoe Self-concept Scale

Name _____

There is a need for each of us to know more about what we are like. This is to help you describe yourself. There are no *right* or *wrong* answers; each person may have different ideas. Answer these according to your feelings. It is important for you to give your own honest answers.

Think carefully and check the answer that tells if you are like the word says 'Nearly Always', About $\frac{1}{2}$ the time', or 'Just Now and Then'.

This is the way I am

	Nearly Always	About $\frac{1}{2}$ the time	Just Now and Then
1 Friendly			
2 Obedient			
3 Honest			
4 Thoughtful			
5 Brave			
6 Careful			
7 Fair			
8 Mean			
9 Lazy			
10 Truthful			
11 Smart			
12 Polite			
13 Clean			
14 Kind			
15 Selfish			
16 Helpful			
17 Good			
18 Cooperative			
19 Cheerful			
20 Jealous			
21 Sincere			
22 Studious			
23 Loyal			
24 Likeable			
25 A good sport			
26 Useful			
27 Dependable			
28 Bashful			
29 Happy			
30 Popular			

Source: J. C. Bledsoe (1967)

general self-concept is located at the top of the hierarchy and specific sub-area self-concepts towards the base. The general self-concept is therefore formed by self-perceptions in the academic, social, emotional and physical domains. In turn, each domain may be sub-divided, as illustrated in Fig. 9 where the academic domain is divided into the areas of the curriculum in which the pupil judges his competence.

A pupil may judge himself to be a good reader, very good at maths and information technology, interested in science but not so good at art or drama. Just as we have explored the academic domain so we can sub-divide the social, emotional and physical domains, but all the time recognising that the four domains are interrelated. In examining the social domain we may recognise qualities we possess, such as, friendliness, trustworthiness, affection, honesty, a sense of humour etc. Each of these social qualities is on a positive–negative continuum and can be measured using a test like Bledsoe Self-concept Scale (Fig. 10).

Finally, consistent with the development of self presented in previous chapters it is emphasised that the self-concept is not passively formed through interaction with the social and physical environment but rather, 'it is a dynamic structure that mediates significant intrapersonal and interpersonal processes' (Schunk, 1990).

The interactive expectations of teachers and pupils

In this section on teacher–pupil expectations some additional related concepts will be examined from an interactionist perspective. They include role and role-set, role-taking, presentation of self and impression management, as each is important in the process of teacher–pupil interaction and bear strongly on a pupil's growing awareness of 'What kind of pupil am I?'

The roles we play are closely related to our conception of self and both develop from the social relationships in which we engage. In a day we each play many roles – mother/father, son/daughter, student, teacher, motorist, shopper and so on; and each role subjects us to particular expectations from other people. In their occupational roles, people are expected to perform the tasks associated with these roles in a prescribed manner, and in their family roles, they are expected to undertake certain familial duties. A role may therefore be defined as a set of expectations impinging upon an individual occupying a social position. In other words, the role an individual plays at any one time determines the 'script' they perform to; and this approach to role uses

Fig. 11: A pupil role-set

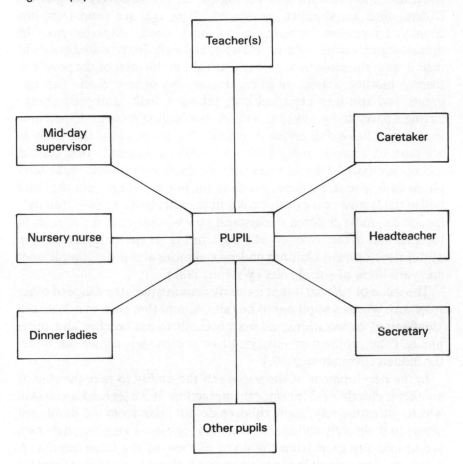

the *dramaturgical* analogy. Thus, role is used not only to give a person's position or status but to determine the nature of the interaction, that is, to prescribe the actions performed in relation to the action–reaction of others. The notion of the role of teacher is meaningless and impossible to define without reference to the reciprocal role of pupil; similarly the role of parent has no meaning except in relation to the role of child. The behaviour appropriate to the roles we occupy are learned as part of the process of socialisation and, in the case of teacher, as a result of specific training.

Most importantly, roles are relational constructs. They have their basis in a particular situation or relationship which prescribes certain styles of relating to others. Many of the roles we play, like the situations and relationships we engage in, are relatively long-term. Others, such as, shopper, passenger, client etc. are short-term but equally have their scripts, props and social expectations. In dramaturgical terms children learn about scripts for repeated events in their lives at the same time as they learn about the roles of the people in them – mother, father, teacher, doctor and others. Some familiar events and routines are mealtime, taking a bath, going shopping, having a party and going to school. A toddler first pretends to perform some act or has a doll perform some act but is not aware that the acts are part of a social role. Later the child understands that certain actions are part of social roles, that mothers buy things, make telephone calls, prepare a meal and clean the house. At age four the child understands how two or three roles fit together and can play 'family'. By age six, most children understand how whole networks of roles fit together – as in the 'role-set' of a pupil in Fig. 11 (p. 109). At each step of this development children understand more about the complexities and variations of social roles (Watson, 1981).

The value of *role-set* is that it clearly demonstrates the range of other roles with which a pupil has to be familiar and that each may hold out 'conflicting' expectations, as may occur between teacher and other pupils. (The problem of satisfying two audiences is drawn out under the hidden curriculum p. 80.)

In the development of the social self the ability to take the role of another is clearly vital for smooth interaction. It is a learned social skill which, unfortunately, some children do not learn from the significant others in their early childhood. *Role-taking* means viewing one's own action and situation from the point of view of the other person. It means putting oneself in the other person's shoes to see things from his perspective. It is a cognitive activity and does not involve acting as the other person does nor does it necessarily involve adopting another person's viewpoint. It is simply an attempt to understand or appreciate it. As we shall see in the following chapter bullies have great difficulty in identifying with their victim's position. For teachers, the whole process of 'good' teaching is reflecting on one's own decisions and actions, to try to see how individual pupil's will respond to the work you set and expectations you hold.

We can extend our dramaturgical approach to social behaviour further in our consideration of role. Like the tragic and comic masks Greek actors wore to identify themselves to their audiences, social actors wear metaphorical masks corresponding to the social roles they are presenting. They act in terms of the set of expectations that define roles, not in a rigid, mechanistic way as if puppets on a string, but by actively presenting themselves using a variety of interactional tactics which produce a convincing performance. The writer Erving Goffman is particularly associated with this approach, which he develops in his aptly titled book *The Presentation of Self in Everyday Life* (1969). The approach is valuable for understanding classroom life too. It is assumed 'that when an individual appears before others he will have many motives for trying to control the impression that they receive of the situation' (Goffman, 1969). Thus, interaction is structured by *impression management*, the process of taking the role of another and organising one's own behaviour so that the other person(s) responds in the way one intended. Nearly all social behaviour involves an element of self-presentation, that is, sending signals about how we each see ourselves and how, in turn, we would like to be regarded and treated. Under normal circumstances we would all wish to present an image that is favourable and in that sense impression management is one method of preserving self-image. Goffman (1969) gives a superb, if fictional account of impression management, in which he describes how Preedy, an Englishman on holiday, makes his first appearance on the beach. What Goffman is drawing our attention to is the way in which Preedy has learned a number of ways of behaving which he believes are socially desirable and which, in an exaggerated way, he sets out to achieve.

But in any case he took care to avoid catching anyone's eye. First of all, he had to make it clear to those potential companions of his holiday that they were of no concern to him whatsoever. He stared through them, round them, over them – eyes lost in space. The beach might have been empty. If by chance a ball was thrown his way, he looked surprised; then let a smile of amusement lighten his face (Kindly Preedy), looked round dazed to see that there were people on the beach, tossed it back with a smile to himself and not a smile at the people, and then resumed carelessly his nonchalant survey of space.

But it was time to institute a little parade, the parade of the Ideal Preedy. By devious handlings he gave anyone who wanted to look a chance to see the title of his book – a Spanish translation of Homer, classic thus, but not daring, cosmopolitan too – and then gathered together his beach-wrap and bag into a neat sand-resistant pile (Methodical and Sensible Preedy), rose slowly to stretch at ease his huge frame (Big-Cat Preedy), and tossed aside his sandals (Carefree Preedy, after all).

(Goffman, 1969)

The above extract usefully illustrates the concept but there is the danger that impression management may be regarded as the act of presenting 'false' selves. In fact, some commentators have criticised Goffman for suggesting that humans are more devious than they really are. But it needs to be emphasised

> that impression management is also used in the service of presenting a true self-image. It is one of life's small tragedies that unless we are careful, people will not get the view of us that we consider to be an accurate one.
>
> (Heiss, 1981)

How are children to know that you are a 'firm but fair' teacher unless you mention things that indicate that this is so or do things that lead them to that conclusion?

From his studies of primary schools Pollard (1986) identified personal interests and concerns which occupy teachers and pupils in the immediacy of their classroom experiences. These 'interests-at-hand' are summarised in Fig. 12 below but it will be evident from Pollard's discussion that in the preservation of self both parties are concerned about managing events to their own best interests and the preservation of self-image.

Fig. 12: Classroom interests-at-hand of teachers and children

Teachers	Children
SELF	SELF
– self-image	– self-image
– workload	– control of stress
– health and stress	– enjoyment
– enjoyment	– dignity
– autonomy	
ORDER	PEER GROUP MEMBERSHIP
INSTRUCTION	LEARNING

Source: Pollard (1986)

> In the case of teachers some common factors which are suggested are: a desire to control the workload involved in teaching, expectation of deriving intrinsic pleasure and enjoyment from classroom life where possible, an attempt to control the level of stress and tension involved in the job, and, more generally and significantly, ambitions to maintain

whatever particular self-image, with regard to teaching, that has been adopted by each teacher. This latter may relate to factors such as educational philosophies, characteristic forms of teaching, levels of commitment, etc. In addition, I found that many primary school teachers tend to want to work within a defined area of autonomy and, where this is established, they will act to maintain and protect it. Teachers' interests-at-hand of order and instruction are in a slightly different category and can be seen as providing a means of maintaining the various facets of self . . . children wish to control the levels of stress which they experience in their classrooms. Stress can be seen both positively and negatively. For instance, some children may see the element of stress which is related to risk taking and mischief as a necessary part of these experiences. On the other hand, most primary school children seek to avoid stress when it is being introduced or imposed by a teacher. Enjoyment is a second major concern for young children, and in the immediacy of their classroom experiences it is a prominent criterion by which such experiences are judged and in response to which new courses of action are contemplated. The maintenance of dignity is a further facet of self. This concern is often under threat from academic criteria in the evaluative contexts which schools provide, but it is also very important to children when teachers seek to control them behaviourally. The way this is done is crucial, with children often responding adversely if they feel themselves to have been humiliated or treated unfairly. The final facet of the interest-at-hand of self which I have identified here is that of self-image. This relates to children's sense of their own identity and to their attempts to sustain and develop it.

(Pollard, 1986)

Teacher expectations of pupils

In the developmental process of a child's growing awareness of self as a pupil an understanding of the reciprocal relationships of teacher and pupil is essential, as each gives meaning to the other's role performance. Initially, we shall discuss the expectancy factor and impression management, then teacher expectation and their consequences for pupils' work and behaviour, and finally, a brief discussion of pupil expectations of teacher. Wherever possible we shall draw upon research carried out in primary schools, although it will be necessary to use data from research with older pupils to support certain points. The emphasis throughout the book is social development but the greater proportion of research into teacher expectation has been into their effect on academic progress. But cognitive and social development in the classroom are not independent of each other, rather they are closely interactive in the personal development of the child. It is also important that we spend time examining teacher expectations in the light of the expressions of concern in certain government quarters about low teacher expectations and depressed pupil outcomes.

The expectancy effect

The expectancy effect pervades social life. Whenever we enter into social interaction with others we carry a range of expectations as to what will happen. Expectations are essential to smooth interpersonal interaction and in typical role-taking behaviour we predict the behaviour of others and adjust our own behaviour accordingly. In this way our expectations define the situation for us and are an important part of a child's social learning. Firstly, our expectations are based on the *social context* – with its functions, props and people who play a given role. Here the person's *position* or status determines our expectations, for example whether it be a shop assistant, police officer, doctor, hairdresser etc. They are members of an identifiable group by occupation, nationality, social class or, in schools, different academic grouping. Secondly, our expectations will be derived from what we know or believe to be true about certain individuals as *people*, for example relatives, friends and neighbours. In these cases, time and proximity have made it possible for us to get to know the person's qualities, personality, habits and so on, from which we predict their behaviour. In the primary school, teachers (and pupils) have the opportunity to get to know each other well, that is, they progress from generalised-position expectations to person-specific expectations.

It is through the expectations of others that we learn what behaviour is approved or disapproved. For example, a teacher may say to a pupil: 'Don't you speak to me like that – you may talk like that at home but not to me!' As we go about our daily lives most of our behaviour is observed by someone; whether it be in our home, in the street, at work, school or play, we are under the scrutiny of other people. Most of the time our behaviour goes unquestioned as it fits into socially approved limits but when we divert from those expectations then our behaviour is brought into question. 'I wonder why he behaved like that?' or 'That's not like you!' Within the mind of the observer he is seeking to understand, explain or even justify why the other person's behaviour does not conform to expectations. (See the section on rules pp. 81–8 for further discussion.)

> And in places like schools; rule-governed organizations, all facets of pupil behaviour are up for assessment; which means that every action must have a justifiable reason – but justifiable within the terms of the organization. If the observed behaviour is seen as legitimate and conforming to the prescribed norms then it is regarded as meaningful, but if it does not follow the social rules and associated motives then it is defined as pointless, meaningless – even irrational. As we make sense of our own world so we dismiss or discredit behaviour that threatens its ordered existence. In schools, where consistent and predictable behaviour is required of large numbers of pupils, acts that deviate from teachers' expectations are labelled as silly or disobedient unless, in the mind of the teacher, an adequate reason is forthcoming. The range, frequency, and intensity of what is labelled disruptive behaviour is wide, extending from talking in class to verbal abuse, from arriving late for a lesson to attacking a teacher.
>
> (Tattum, 1982)

In education the expectancy effect is believed to operate when teachers expect certain pupils to perform at levels above or below average. Those expectations will then influence the teachers' behaviour towards the relevant pupil such that the expectations come true. At this point we need to interject a cautionary word, as interpersonal perception and communications are much more complexed than a simple linear causation. Rogers (1982) offers a four stage process to demonstrate how teacher expectancy effect may progress.

(1) Teachers must form an impression and so establish future expect-
    ations.
(2) The behaviour of the teacher must be affected by that impression.
(3) Pupils must notice the teachers' affected behaviour.
(4) Pupils must respond to the teacher's behaviour in a manner that
    closely matches the teacher's expectations.

Teacher expectation and pupil development

Teacher expectation is of paramount importance in our examination of the social education and personal development of pupils. In the first instance, it is associated with the way a child gradually comes to see himself as a pupil and whether his self-evaluation is positive or negative. Secondly, the expectancy process draws upon two other central concepts, namely, the *self-fulfilling prophecy* and *labelling*. Another reason why teacher evaluation is so important is because it contains the definition and expectation of a significant other whose assessment, in the context of school, is very difficult for a child to challenge. Thus, pupils accept teacher's judgements and so come to behave in accordance with her definitions. This process is the self-fulfilling prophecy.

For pupils to learn in school it is self-evident that they need sufficient self-confidence in themselves and their abilities to make an effort to succeed. Without self-confidence some pupils will expect the worst in every situation and will be constantly afraid of doing or saying the wrong thing. People high in their own estimation approach tasks and people with the expectation that they will be well-received and successful. But pupils who are labelled unmotivated, lazy, inattentive, become reluctant to take the risk of further damaging exposures. Early research by Zimmerman and Allebrand (1968) demonstrated that poor readers lack a sense of personal worth and adequacy to the point that they actively avoid achievement. For poor readers to work hard and still fail provides painful proof of their inadequacy. To avoid such proof, many pupils deliberately choose not to try. Their defence against failure is to accept themselves as failures. From their position it is better not to read at all than to read badly and face embarrassment and humiliation. As Glock (1972) succinctly expressed it, 'A negative self-image is its own best defender.'

Labelling and grouping can exacerbate the development of a negative self-concept, particularly as many categories are powerful instruments for social regulation and control. In Tattum (1982) the labelling process was examined with reference to disruptive pupils who had been transferred to special units. (Earlier, in Chapter 3, the development of negative pupil careers was discussed.)

> The establishment of units and the mechanisms for the selection and transfer of pupils have confirmed the category in the consciousness of teachers and pupils alike. Categories are not pre-existent but are socially constructed so that people may classify others, and before anyone can be seen as deviant there must be a category to which he or she can be assigned – the official establishment of units facilitates the public labelling process of disrupters. Physical segregation and isolation from 'normal' people is an extreme confirmatory act in the minds of both definers and defined. Pupils earned reputations for being difficult, disobedient, or aggressive prior to the creation of units but it was contained within the school; the education system has taken a

major step such that it can now identify and name this new category of pupil by a process which contains all the characteristics of public stigmatization.

(Tattum, 1982)

The potency of labelling is effective when it is accepted as part of the labelled person's own definition of self and he adopts the role.

When a person begins to employ his deviant behaviour or a role based on it as a means of defence, attack or adjustment to the overt and covert problems created by the consequent societal reaction to him, his deviation is secondary.

(Lemert, 1951)

The value of Lemert's distinction between *primary deviation*, which is rule-breaking we all engage in at one time or another, and *secondary deviation*, is three-fold: firstly, it reiterates the earlier point that labels can be resisted; secondly, it makes the link between the label and self-concept; and thirdly, it emphasises the part played by the labeller(s). Negative labels can degrade, hurt, exclude non-conformists and justify all manner of behaviour towards the labelled person. Rist (1970) claims that many children are 'locked in' to a particular life style, treatment and self-evaluation by early labelling as slow-learner, hyperactive, maladjusted, disrupter, poor reader, no good at sums, clumsy or, as happened in our story on p. 56 'the dandelion table'.

It is not only natural but professionally required that teachers have expectations of the children in their classes. Dangers arise when expectations are based on flimsy or false information, and especially, when they shape and control a pupil's educational career. When children arrive in the reception class it is not unreasonable for the teacher to expect that the children will know their own name and address; recognise letters, numbers, colours and shapes; to be able to toilet themselves, hang their clothes up, dress themselves and put their shoes on. Unfortunately, not all homes prepare them in these and other academic and social skills.

According to Rogers (1982), teachers hold two *broad types of expectations*. Those that relate directly to the pupil's academic capabilities and those that are concerned with social characteristics. These types of expectations have positive or negative connotations for subsequent teacher behaviour. Rogers proceeds to identify two categories of teacher behaviour:

(1) *administrative behavioural effects* and
(2) *interactive behavioural effects*.

The former includes actions such as academic grouping, curricular choices and even, teaching style – the many aspects of the hidden curriculum discussed in Chapter 4. The latter category includes verbal and non-verbal communication, plus the quantity and quality of teacher–pupil interactions. The following pieces of research by Rist (1970) and Pidgeon (1970) demonstrate administrative effects, whilst Brophy and Good's work over many years illustrate the interactive effects of teacher behaviour.

Rist (1970)

Rist's observations in the classroom of a black American kindergarten teacher and her thirty black pupils, found that 'permanent' seating arrangements made on the eighth day of school coincided with the social class of the children. The teacher grouped the children at three tables, explaining that they were seated according to their ability to 'learn'. Observations revealed that the groups received differential treatment and experiences. The lowest group received more control-orientated teacher communications, had less interaction with the teacher, and received more ridicule from the other pupils in the class. The children in the top group were from families with higher incomes and education levels; were better dressed, neater and cleaner; talked and interacted more easily with the teacher and received more positive responses and privileges from her. At the end of the year the children's IQ was tested and whilst some children from Table 2 and 3 had higher scores than some children on Table 1 they retained the 'ability' grouping assigned to them on day eight of schooling when they moved to the next class. This ability grouping was reinforced in first grade and followed the pupils into second grade. The wider question is the extent to which such initial administrative decisions and treatment – based on social and not educational criteria – helped to predetermine the school careers of children.

Pidgeon (1970)

The value of Pidgeon's study is that it demonstrates both positive and negative outcomes from administrative decisions. For various reasons, a group of primary children whose birthdays fell at a certain time of the year, were kept in their primary schools while their classmates transferred on to secondary school. The children were given intelligence and attainment tests before the move and some took a similar battery of tests a year later. Comparison of the test scores showed that the children who had stayed in their primary schools consistently made gains in test scores, while those who had moved to secondary school consistently made losses. It must be remembered that the decision about transfer had been made according to date of birth and not ability.

Pidgeon recognised that there may be a number of reasons for the different performances but his preferred explanation is in the different attitudes and expectations for the pupils' development conveyed by the teachers in the different types of schools.

Brophy and Good (1970, 1974)

Interactive effects between teacher and pupil can come about through verbal and non-verbal signals. Brophy and Good suggest that differential treatment emerges through the frequency and quality of verbal contacts. Teachers tend to communicate low expectations to pupils by calling on low-achievers less frequently than high-achievers. Even when the pupil volunteers an answer, he or she is less likely to be chosen than a high achieving pupil. More striking instances of the way teachers communicate their expectations lie in the quality of verbal exchanges. Some teachers praise any response a low achieving pupil gives regardless of accuracy or correctness, which does little to develop academic self-esteem or credibility with peers. Other teachers, on the other hand, are overly critical and are more likely to criticise an incorrect answer from a low-achiever than a high-achiever. The disproportionate amount of criticism given these pupils conveys a message that they are failures.

> the situation is clear for lows in certain classes: if they respond, they are more likely to be criticized and less likely to be praised; thus, the safest strategy is to remain silent and hope that the teacher will call on someone else.
>
> (Brophy and Good, 1974)

When Brophy and Good informed the teachers about these patterns they changed their behaviour so that the pupils were treated more equally, which had the effect of bringing about an improvement in the behaviour and achievement of the low achievers.

John Holt (1969) describes similar pupil behaviours in his book *How Children Fail* and Cranfield and Wells (1976) use the term 'killer statements' to describe the means whereby another person's negative comments or behaviour can damage a child's self-esteem. Teachers have been heard to say things like – 'I'm not going to waste my time on someone as stupid as you'; 'You are an idiot!'; and 'Wrong again!'.

> The non-verbal message lies in the teacher's tone of voice, physical appearance, body stance, facial expression, gestures and physical proximity. Eye contact, especially looking directly at a particular student, can signal, 'I am sincere in what I say, and my words are aimed directly at you.' A warm tone of voice, a neat physical appearance, a friendly smile, and direct eye contact all communicate that the student really is accepted. A teacher's aloof behaviour, forced smile, tightly crossed arms, or indifferent manner may say more clearly than words, 'I don't care for you'.
>
> Students are quick to spot conflicts between what teachers say and what their non-verbal behaviour communicates. It is easy to lie to a pupil verbally about their performance and your acceptance of them. It is almost impossible to lie with non-verbal signs; they make real feelings obvious.
>
> (Burns, 1982)

The sources of teacher expectations can be both *direct* and *indirect*. Direct information would come from teacher interpretation of such characteristics as age, sex, social background, race, attainment records. Each of these characteristics may not have an effect on its own but in conjunction with others may fit into the teacher's scheme of the 'ideal' pupil. Indirect sources would include parents, other teachers, educational psychologists, education welfare officers. Examples of direct and indirect sources come from the work of Garwood and McDavid (1975), Palardy (1969) and Rosenthal and Jacobson (1968).

Garwood and McDavid (*1975*)

This study is included to demonstrate the flimsy nature of some information used, as it demonstrates how teachers had stereotypes related to first names. Boys named David were viewed as good, strong, wise, active, complex, sociable, excitable and masculine. The same teachers viewed Harold as signifying weak, bad, foolish, passive, humorous, simple, unsociable and calm. Desirable names included Craig, James, John, Jonathan and Patrick, whilst Bernard, Donald, Horace, Jerome, Roderick and Maurice were regarded as undesirable. Garwood (1976), in a further study, found that boys bearing first names judged desirable by teachers tended to have more positive self-concept and score higher in their attainment than those with undesirable names.

Similar research by Harari and McDavid (1973) also pointed to the direct influence of the name-stereotype phenomenon in schooling. They asked experienced teachers to grade children's essays (previously judged as neither good nor bad, but of a comparable standard) which were linked to authorship by a chosen desireable–undesirable first name. Essays written by students with desirable names were scored significantly higher than the same essays carrying undesirable names. The authors saw evidence of teacher expectancy at work.

Palardy (1969)

The Palardy investigation looks at the relationship between expectations and sex-typing. The author asked 63 first-grade teachers to report on their beliefs about the rate at which first-grade boys learn to read. From the 42 teachers who responded to the questionnaire he identified a group of 5 teachers who believed that boys were almost as good as girls at learning to read and another group of 5 who thought that boys were only half as good as girls. The pupils came from similar family backgrounds and a reading pre-test administered to all children showed no differences among them. On the post-test, however, boys taught by teachers who believed that they were almost as good as girls had progressed as well as the girls in their reading, whilst boys taught by teachers who thought that girls were superior scored significantly lower than girls. These results suggest that pupil performance can be depressed as well as raised by teacher expectations. Palardy concluded that a self-fulfilling prophecy was in evidence, that is, the teachers' beliefs actually influenced the outcomes.

Rosenthal and Jacobson (1968)

In their famous study, Rosenthal and Jacobson set out to address the expectancy question, that is, do children perform better when their teacher expects them to. The research demonstrates how an *indirect* source of information can influence teacher behaviour.

The school chosen for the study was 'Oak School', an elementary school located in an urban working-class San Francisco community. Every child was given an intelligence test, one which the researchers purported would predict 'intellectual blooming' during the coming year. The teachers then were led to believe a number of the pupils in their class would improve more than the rest of their pupils but, in fact, the researchers had selected 20 per cent of the children entirely at random. There was no reason to believe that they would perform any better, unless their teacher's expectations brought this about. At the end of the first year the 'bloomers' had gained significantly more IQ points relative to the other children. Although this was due mainly to changes in one first-grade class where the 'bloomers' improved by 15 IQ points. There was no significant gains for grades three to six. Nevertheless, Rosenthal and Jacobson believed that they had demonstrated expectancy effects and speculated on the reasons:

> Teachers may have treated their children in a more pleasant, friendly, and encouraging fashion when they expected greater intellectual gains of them ... Such communications together with possible changes in teaching technique may have helped the child to learn by changing his self-concept image, his expectations of his own behaviour, and his motivation, as well as his cognitive style and skills.
>
> (Rosenthal and Jacobson, 1968)

On social outcomes, the teachers were asked at the end of the first year to rate their pupils on a number of behavioural criteria. 'Bloomers' were considered to be significantly more curious, interesting, appealing and happy, to have a greater chance of future success and to be less in need of approval.

This study has been subjected to extensive scrutiny and criticism, also, many researchers have tried to replicate their work with varying degrees of success. Detailed discussion of the criticism and replication can be found in Rogers (1982).

Earlier in this chapter we made the distinction between *academic and social expectations*, although cautioning against regarding them as independent of each other rather than interrelated. Some researchers suggest that the social impression a teacher has of a pupil is the more effective in teacher–pupil interaction, and we will discuss studies which support this view. For example, in the Rosenthal and Jacobson (1968) study there were indications that teachers were more aware of the social characteristics of the 'bloomers' and regarded them as 'nicer' to teach. Rogers (1982) provides a well developed analysis of the interactive nature of academic and social expectations:

> When a child first attends school a teacher has very little information available regarding that child's academic potential. What she does have available is a certain amount of information regarding the extent to which the child is likely to be pleasant to work with. It is suggested

that it is these more social expectations that initially determine the type of teacher-initiated teacher–pupil interactions that take place. These interactions, in turn, give rise to various other effects that produce higher levels of performance from the 'nicer' children. These higher levels of performance become part of the general pool of information that becomes available to later teachers of the same child. Having done better, the 'nicer' children will be expected to do better in the future. However, these later (in terms of the child's school career) expectations will come to have less and less of a biasing role and more and more of a maintaining role. Having already done well, a child is likely to be placed on the top tables, in the higher streams, go to the 'better' schools and so on.

(Rogers, 1982)

Rogers (1982) proceeds to argue that a 'clear distinction should be made between the self-fulfilling effects that an expectation might have and the expectation-maintaining effects that an expectation might have'. In other words, comfortable matching in teacher social expectations and pupil social behaviour provides teacher with complimentary role partners with whom she can relate. From interviews with Chicago teachers Becker (1952) describes their ideal pupil as one who is eager to learn, well behaved, neatly dressed – and, most importantly, did not offend the teacher's moral propriety.

Two studies that provide evidence in support of the teacher-expectancy effect in the social domain are Beez (1968) and Crano and Mellon (1978).

Beez (1968)

Beez had 60 graduate students teach the meanings of a series of pictorial signs, on a one-to-one basis, to five to six year olds on a Head Start programme. Each teacher was given a faked psychological profile to read, in which the child was described as of normal intelligence and capable of benefiting from the programme because of personality characteristics. Other children were described as of low-average intelligence and not well adjusted to school. The high ability were described as being open and friendly, smiling readily, well motivated and so on. The lower-ability ones were described as sulky, unresponsive and untidily dressed.

Supplied with false academic and social data the teachers of high-ability children attempted to teach nearly twice as many signs as teachers of low-ability children. The first group also learned a significantly greater number of signs with 77 per cent of them learning five or more signs compared with the low-ability pupils. Higher-ability children were also rated by their teachers as being more intelligent, more socially competent and having a higher level of attainment. Accepting that they were students and not teachers, we do have an example of how indirect data can raise or lower expectations and hence, pupil learning achievements. Furthermore, the student-teachers also proceeded to make social evaluations of the children's personal qualities.

Crano and Mellon (1978)

Crano and Mellon used data collected earlier in Barker Lunn's (1970) study of streaming in primary schools in England and Wales. A group of seven year olds had been tested on reading, arithmetic, as well as IQ, over three years. In addition, the teachers in each year were asked to provide personal assessments of their pupils in two domains. On the *academic domain* they provided an over-all assessment of each child's general ability and predicted their chances of gaining a grammar school place. On the *social domain* teachers gave their views on each child's attitude towards school, behaviour and social acceptance within the class.

The clearest finding to emerge was that the social expectations of the first year teachers were causally predominant over the attainments of the same pupils in their second year. In fact, their data indicated that in eight of the twelve cases the pupils took their year one teachers' perceptions of them to their next class and that these self-perceptions became the expectation of the standard two teachers. In the remaining four cases the reverse occurred. The second year teachers made their own formulations of the children rather than permit individual and class behaviour to continue from the previous year's social expectations.

The debate between passing on records and the 'clean-slate' philosophy is part of staffroom chat. That we keep careful records of children's behaviour and performance is important but teachers must be alert to the consequences for the pupil of negative labels which may follow a child throughout his schooling. For in the Crano and Mellon investigation the earlier expectations followed the children into the next class and affected their behaviour – both positively and negatively. Commenting on their findings Rogers observes,

Their results, however, suggest that, particularly with social expectations held by teachers for young children, the expectations have a relatively greater effect upon the attainments than vice versa, and that over-all expectations tended to determine performance.

(Rogers, 1982)

Pupils' expectations of teachers

The social side of schooling is important for the social education and personal development of children. They learn from teachers and also from their peers, as we shall more fully develop in the next chapter. School is an opportunity to meet with friends, to gossip, play games, make swops, discuss the latest 'craze', and much more. Moreover, children observe teachers at work more than they observe any other occupation – they are experts on teachers. Therefore, we must not be surprised if they 'weigh-up' teachers, 'suss them out', test them and hold expectations about the types of teachers they like and respect. Unfortunately, we have very little research data on pupil's perception of teachers – especially children of primary school age. Meighan (1978) found that headteachers were unwilling to permit pupil assessment of students in training on the grounds that 'pupils have little of value to say or will abuse the opportunity to comment'. In fact, he found the majority of comments to be positive, sympathetic and balanced, with few abusive or malicious remarks.

An early investigation of pupils' perceptions and expectations of their teachers was carried out by Nash (1974). In his investigation of pupils' perceptions of their teachers Nash used a method based on Kelly's personal construct theory. A class of Scottish twelve year olds were given individually a set of cards on which the names of their teachers were printed. The pupils were then asked to make two piles of the cards according to whether (a) he 'got on with', or (b) he 'didn't get on with' a teacher. One card from each set was then chosen and shown to the child who was asked to explain in what ways the behaviour of the two teachers differed. On analysis Nash found that the six constructs, or pairs of descriptive terms, that emerged most frequently were:

(1) Keeps order   Unable to keep order
(2) Teaches you   Doesn't teach you
(3) Explains   Doesn't explain
(4) Interesting   Boring
(5) Fair   Unfair
(6) Friendly   Unfriendly

An analysis of these findings showed that teachers with whom the pupils failed to get on were those who fell short of their expectations – and this related both to academic and social expectations. The more closely teachers approximated to the positive column the more acceptable was the behaviour of the pupils.

An interesting study by Kutnick (1983) illustrates the developmental quality of pupils' expectations as they progress from infants to top juniors. The reception class children described teachers as being similar to their own parents, that is, they were adults in school who looked after their basic needs. But after a year of school experience pupil perception of teacher changed to being someone more closely related to daily classroom organisation, in that they helped with reading and writing, handed out equipment, and organised play. By the time they entered the junior school children were much more aware of the disproportionate power relations that exist in classrooms. The children expected teachers to keep control as well as teach. In top juniors the children became more aware of the expectation of the other members of the class and so negotiated to satisfy both audiences. Throughout primary school the majority of children enjoy school and get on well with their teachers. The picture changes somewhat for some youngsters as they transfer to secondary school and enter a more turbulent period of adolescence.

Yet, despite these changes, secondary school pupils continue to emphasise the personal and social role of teachers. Quine (1974) observed that in addition to instrumental and, not surprisingly, vocational values, pupils also strongly attached social and emotional values to school. In a survey of the attitudes towards secondary school held by thirteen and fourteen year olds, Weston *et al.* (1978) found that 'teachers could do more than merely hold the ring in this area (the personal and social) while vocational goals are pursued.' Regardless of social background and ability, pupils expected teachers to assist them in their personal and social development and to create a happy and supportive school ethos.

The social side of schooling is also emphasised by Woods (1978) in a study of the views of over 200 fourth and fifth-year secondary modern pupils on the relationship between the quality of work required and the personal qualities of the teacher. As senior pupils they distinguished between examination and non-examination work but in the final analysis work is about relationships and Woods comments, 'The simple moral is to make work count, and for teachers to be human.' Pupils do look for the 'human face' of teachers, as Wright's (1962) findings confirm. She found that what pupils find lacking in teachers are the very qualities that make them human. In comparison with other adults, pupils rated teachers more favourably on their primary role qualities such as being interesting, wise, successful – but hard. On qualities such as kindness, fairness and warmth, which are judged on the basis of social expectations, they were rated less favourably.

We conclude this section on pupil expectation by looking at Halperin's (1976) research. She sets out to relate the classroom perceptions of six year olds to the beliefs and behaviour of their teachers. Following interviews the teachers were classified as being either academic or social in their general educational aims. Academic teacher aims were instrumental as their emphasis was on an early grasp of the basics, particularly reading. Social teachers were more concerned about the expressive domain, that is, ensuring that their children had adjusted to the demands of the classroom.

One of Halperin's findings was that to a large extent the teachers' attitudes towards schooling helped to determine the attitudes of their pupils. In interviews children were asked to name the pupil who, in their opinion, the teacher thought to be the best. There was significantly greater agreement within the classes of academic teachers than was the case in the classes of social teachers. From teacher behaviour they had learned the competitive aspect of schooling in which the best children were highly praised, received rewards and had their work displayed. The teacher had defined the situation and her expectations influenced pupil perception of what it meant to be a pupil. The social teachers held a different philosophy in which cooperation was more in evidence, such that their pupils did not relate on best–worse evaluations.

When writing about teacher expectations there is a danger that in concentrating on the negative effects of labelling and the self-fulfilling prophecy, we can give the impression that teachers are insensitive to the effects they have on the children they teach. This would be a gross exaggeration. It may be true of some but not of the great majority. The dilemma for teachers who are aware of the negative impact of some of the things they do and say in the immediacy of classroom interaction, is to present themselves in a way more likely to give all pupils equal opportunities to develop socially and academically. Burns (1982) offers four ways to counteract the negative aspects of the expectancy factor.

They are not easy to accomplish but are basic reminders for a busy day:

(1) interact evenly with all pupils;
(2) talk with all pupils;
(3) praise pupils realistically;
(4) set tasks to suit individuals.

Exercises

(1) Construct your personal academic profile along the lines illustrated in Fig. 9.
(2) Complete the Twenty Statement Test – 'Who am I?' (p. 102). You may consider repeating it towards the end of the academic year and see the measure of consistency.
(3) List three roles you play which are important to you. How do you see yourself in each role, for example parent or student? Is there consistency between them? What self-image and self-esteem do they contain?
(4) You may wish to draw up your own list of desirable–undesirable first names for boys and girls. Then discuss what characteristics you associate with some examples.
(5) Fill in the blocks in Fig. 8 'Multiple sources of self-image and self-esteem', with both positive and negative evaluations.

Additional reading

1. For a further development of labelling and self-fulfilling prophecy see Tattum (1982), pp. 66–9 and 184–5.
2. For a detailed discussion of the replications and criticisms of *Pygmalion in the Classroom* by Rosenthal and Jacobson (1968), see Colin Rogers (1982) pp. 19–37.
3. Burns (1982) pp. 243–7, gives a detailed account of the ways to counter the negative aspects of the expectancy factor.
4. Burns, R. B. (1979) *The Self Concept* Longman, London, is an excellent source book on the measurement of the self-concept.
5. Craske, M. L. (1988) 'Learned helplessness, self-worth, motivation and attribution retraining for primary school children', *British Journal of Educational Psychology*, 58, 152–64.

CHAPTER 6

Peer Relationships and Social Development

In this chapter we shall deal with peer relationships and friendships because, as children grow older, the influence of peers increases, and moreover, friendships are very dear to children. We will then discuss play and its importance to child development before progressing to looking at playtime in the school playground. There is a growing interest in making playgrounds more interesting and stimulating for pupils, thus making playtime a more constructive time in the school day. It is believed that this is one way of reducing indiscipline both in the playground and classroom. On the theme of indiscipline, we shall look at bullying behaviour and how aggressive pupils can make playtime an unhappy experience for some children.

Friendship and peer relationships

As children develop socially they deal more frequently and with greater sophistication with those who make up their social world. They form relationships with adults beyond their immediate family and play with other children. They come to understand the complexities of social interaction, and how others affect them and they, in turn, affect others. As the child progresses through primary school, friends become more and more important. They are important sources of companionship and recreation, someone with whom you share advice and valued possessions, are confidants, critics and allies and provide support in times of stress and transition to a new class or school. By the final year of primary school, ten-year-olds consider friendship to be a sharing of inner thoughts and feelings. They understand that a friend is a special person with whom you enjoy mutual respect and affection. In this way children realise that acts of friendship could change a person's feelings from lonely and sad to being wanted and happy – as is the case with many victims of bullying. It is because friends become so important to a child's well-being at this age that many, when asked about their anxieties about transfer to secondary school, name being separated from friends as a major cause of worry. In America, Berndt (1982) has reported that friendships generally are disrupted by the transition to junior high school and that youngsters with close friendships adjust more successfully to their new school. This is clearly a good reason for primary and receiving secondary schools working together to try to place every new pupil in a class with one close friend. The same recommendation applies to the seating arrangements permitted by teachers on receiving a new class at the beginning of the school year.

It is possible that peer relationships play an even more important role today than in the past. The increasing number of working mothers and one-parent families has resulted in earlier entry of young children into organised peer group settings such as day-care centres and nursery schools. Furthermore, children today participate more frequently in out-of-school activities such as cubs and brownies, church groups and organised leisure activities. These experiences guarantee that children spend considerable time with same-age peers throughout childhood. Therefore, it is very important that a child enjoys close friendships and learns the social skills necessary to negotiate successful entry into the various social worlds available.

Children operate in two social worlds, that of child–adult relationships and then the world of peer relations. The major distinction between these worlds is the quality of equality, for children who are at similar stages of cognitive, physical, emotional and social maturity interact as co-equals.

In his writings, Piaget (1926, 1932) noted that it is the cooperation and mutuality operative in peer relationships that allows children to gain broader cognitive perspectives about their social worlds. Piaget considered very young children to be egocentric and neither able nor willing to take the perspectives of their social partners, that is, they had not learned the social skills of role-taking. However, he suggested that with the onset of peer play, a unique opportunity occurs to establish egalitarian and reciprocal relationships, as well as experience conflict and negotiation. Such conflict and negotiation, whether involving objects or alternative perspectives, were thought to contain the power of eliciting compromise and reciprocity. Encounters with peers were thought to bring about the realisation that positive and productive social interaction is gained through cooperation with and sensitivity to one's social partner or friend. The importance of perspective taking cannot be over-emphasised as one of the social skills young children need to learn and in that respect schools are especially able to provide such learning opportunities. As far as bullying is concerned, young children need to be introduced to seeing the act of bullying from the victim's viewpoint and, hence, show them more sympathy and support.

Sullivan (1953) also considered peer relationships to play a significant role in child development. His central tenet was that an individual's personality was shaped by the individual's social relationships, that is, in SI terms – the Self is Social. He maintained that in children of primary school age peers provided the framework for the child's growing understanding of (a) social rules for cooperation and competition and (b) a range of social roles. In pre-adolescence Sullivan speculated that peers, and especially close friendship relationships, foster 'genuine' development in the conceptualisation of equality, mutuality and reciprocity as central characteristics of intimate relationships. Peers can also serve as control agents for each other by punishing or ignoring unacceptable behaviour and reinforcing culturally appropriate behaviour. Hartup (1983) demonstrates how prosocial, aggressive and sex-typed behaviours, among others, can be modified by exposure to peer models. All of which leads us to the conclusion that peer interaction and peer relationships are important forces in the development of social competences during childhood.

Maxwell (1990) provides a summary of many of the points discussed so far relating to the specific development functions of peer relationships. They are:

(1) Socialisation through which the child learns to control aggressive and sexual impulses in socially acceptable ways. This is achieved through negotiation to resolve conflict resulting from unacceptable behaviour, which is essential if a friendship is to continue.

(2) Peers are an important source of a child's self-image and self-esteem, that is, his view of himself. Through the reactions of others a child receives feedback, he also makes direct comparisons against the skills and attributes of age-mates.

(3) From the peer group a child derives a set of values and attitudes, which may conflict with those of adults. In the final years of primary school children begin to come under the influence of teenage culture in all its forms.

(4)   Finally, it is suggested that young children learn higher level social skills from interaction with peers, that is, skills which make them acceptable friends, companions and work-mates in a wide range of adolescent and adult settings.

Reference has already been made to the social function of schooling and Davies (1982) suggests that in addition to having 'best friends' a child may also have 'contingency friends' to turn to in case their closest friend is not available. In her study of Australian primary school pupils she shows how children develop rules of friendship just as they develop rules for assessing teachers. A friend was regarded as someone who was sensible and loyal, who knew how to cooperate and who would share their personal world with you. With a friend the relationship is on an equality basis and provides a basic sense of security. Frowned upon behaviour included 'showing-off', because that aims to elevate the person and put you down. 'Teasing' too can upset the feeling of security, whilst, for older pupils, not 'splitting' or 'grassing' was an important rule in their code of honour. This latter point partly explains why children are unwilling to tell on class-mates who bully, even though they may disapprove of or be on the receiving end of a bully's aggression.

Within the literature on peer relations there has been increasing recognition that friendship and overall group acceptance may constitute distinct and independent aspects of a child's social world. Bukowski and Hoza (1989) have argued that having a friend (a close, mutual, dyadic relationship with a peer) and being popular (being liked or accepted by members of one's peer group) have independent effects on a child's feelings of self-worth. Maxwell (1990) states that 'The two concepts are clearly distinct' and Rubin (1980) warned against the uncritical promotion of popularity as a desirable end in itself, as it may result in an emphasis on superficial relationships and unhealthy competition. Children who are not popular may well have close rewarding friendships with one or two others, whilst a child who is popular may lack one close, intimate friend and the benefits that may come from higher quality peer relationships. For example, research by McGuire and Weisz (1982) indicates a relationship between having a close friend and greater social sensitivity to the needs and feelings of others. To distinguish between the benefits of friendships and popularity carries an important message for teachers and parents, and both should seek to create opportunities for their pupils/children to interact with friends in a deep and sustained way.

For example, schools should spell out to parents the value of their child having a close friend and encourage them to invite children in the neighbourhood to their home, not just for parties but for general play and excursions to places of interest. Equally parents should be advised to take an interest in the social life of their child in school – not just academic progress. They should talk to them about who they play with, eat their lunch with, walk to and from school with and so on. From the school's side teachers too should create situations which help deepen friendships. One successful scheme used by the authors was to get children who live close to each other to draw a plan of their route to and from school, noting names of streets, prominent buildings and other landmarks.

Children can also derive social and personal benefits from being members of a gang. Pollard (1985) provides an example of three groups and their behaviour in classroom and playground – he calls them Goodies, Jokers and Gangs. The goodie groups in his study saw themselves as sensible, honest, quiet and friendly, and would distance themselves from mainstream activities in the playground. Jokers also thought of themselves as sensible but liked to be active both in the classroom and in the playground – their cooperative activities bonded the group. The gang groups were mainly children who were relative failures in academic terms and spent their time 'causing trouble' in one way or another. They regarded the other groups as 'big-heads' or 'show-offs'. Pollard saw considerable evidence of inter-group rivalry, which served to generate in-group solidarity.

For teachers, the value of being party to the culture of pupilhood has been developed by Woods (1983), when he suggests that there are three common themes embedded in the culture that children create in schools: they are relationships, competence and status. The evidence discussed so far would indicate that pupil culture is highly structured by social rules and conventions, and to negotiate successfully requires considerable social sophistication and competence. This point is supported by Davies (1982) who learned from her interviews with upper primary children that when considering appropriate–inappropriate behaviour they were more concerned with consistency within given situations than consistency of action for individuals. She explains children's emphasis on observing situational rules thus:

This detailed awareness of the definition of the situation and its power to dictate appropriate behaviour may well be associated with the fact that school children experience frequent and regular changes of situation over which they have little control. They must pay close attention to the requirements of any one situation such that within its own terms it becomes predictable. Once a situation is predictable, then competent, appropriate behaviour is possible. Censure must fall on those who threaten the reading of each situation. Friends behave in predictable ways towards each other, thereby providing a secure arena for competent behaviour. The children have developed a complex culture centred around these friendships, a culture they recognise as having little to do with the adult world, but which they recognise as having much to do with being a child.

(Davies, 1982)

Returning to the early point made by Woods (1983), he demonstrates how peer groups contribute to a child's development of self. Peer *relationships* are a child's extra-curricular life and foster a feeling of belonging and a sense of identity. *Competence* relates to the previous theme as it illustrates how 'boys and girls are in the process of carving out acceptable identities for themselves'. In order to display competence they must master the social skills of negotiating entry into group activities, manage conflicts and present an acceptable view of self. *Status* is the outcome of the successful management of friendship relations and social competence. In this way it relates to the particular identity a child has developed and acquired, and it has to be worked at and competed for in the pecking-order of peer interaction.

Reputations are cultivated, made, confirmed, sometimes pre-ordained, and jealously guarded. To be 'top of the class', 'best at football', or to possess some other great skill at perhaps art, music or drama, will give kudos among pupils who conform to the school's value system. Some pupils will work hard, not for intrinsic satisfaction, but to improve their performance rating against their fellows – for position rather than performance. As one high-achieving thirteen-year-old boy told me, 'I would like to work for the fun of it, but they [his friends] won't let you. If they beat you, they tease you, they go "ha! ha! ha! I beat you" and you do the same thing to them. I would rather get 49% and come top than we all get 90% . . . You get a reputation which you have to try to keep up, and sometimes that's very hard'.

(Woods, 1983)

Thus children have their own culture and when children arrive at school they are thrown on their own resources to make sense of and negotiate entry into this complex social world. Teachers spell out the rules of acceptable classroom behaviour but know little of the rules of acceptable playtime behaviour. For the child there are shared meanings and understandings which must be mastered if the playground culture is to make sense and be successfully managed. But until children have made friends they cannot participate in pupil culture and so to make and retain a friendship is vitally important.

Bossert (1987) helps us make some links between teacher classroom organisation and the formation of friendship groups. He studied the organisation of four teachers in an American private school serving upper middle-class families – the children were nine years old. Two teachers, Hunt and Field, ran formal classrooms and favoured tight teacher control, whilst the other two, Stone and Park, expected the children to be more self-directed and to work on small group projects. In the formal classes children gradually identified with other children performing at a similar academic level, whilst in the less formal class achievement level did not affect friendships or work group choices. By the eighth week of term all the groups in Hunt and Field's classes worked, ate lunch and played only with pupils achieving at the same level, and these friendship groups remained constant throughout the remainder of Bossert's classroom observation. When interviewed half of the children specifically mentioned academic performance as a criterion for selecting friends.

In the classes of Stone and Park multi-task activities was the norm so that few public comparisons were made and there was very little competition. The range of activities increased the opportunities for children to interact freely with other members of the class, and so peer relations were fluid and independent of relative academic performances. They 'seemed to change friendship groups as often as interests in projects or hobbies changed'. Only one pupil mentioned academic performance as a reason for selecting friends.

> The consistency in forms of peer group structures, both between classrooms having similar instructional organizations and within the same classroom over the two-year study period, as well as the friendship shifts that occurred among students who changed classroom types, demonstrates the impact of the organization of instruction. The varying importance that academic performance played in the selection of friends and workmates cannot be attributed to differences among the children. These pupils adapted readily to the influence of task and reward structures and responded to the dominant organization present in their current classroom.
>
> (Bossert, 1987)

In other words, the organisation of classroom work patterns specifies who interacts with whom and so affects peer relationships within both classroom and playground. Consequently, teachers can shape social interaction for academic reasons but in so doing have an impact on friendship patterns in a way in which they may not be fully cognisant.

Play and playtime

Play is one of those 'taken-for-granted' words which adults freely apply to children's activities, without really thinking what constitutes play. In fact, play is many things and it is a matter of contention whether certain behaviours constitute play. For example, would there be agreement about whether a child painting or model making or even reading constitutes play. Some would argue that the distinction may not depend on the activity but on the attitude of the person involved and the meaning it has for her or him. In this sense play can include leisure and recreational activities, which are voluntarily engaged in for enjoyment. Yet, despite this lack of agreement, play has come to be regarded as beneficial for child development. The 'play ethic' regards it as important for a child's intellectual and aesthetic development, and for social and personal growth. This view was emphasised by the Plowden Report (1967):

> We now know that play – in the sense of 'messing about' either with material objects or with other children, and of creating fantasies – is vital to children's learning and therefore vital in school. Adults who criticize teachers for allowing children to play are unaware that play is the principal means of learning in early childhood.
>
> (Plowden Report, 1967)

In an attempt to categorise different forms of play Piaget (1951) distinguished between 'practice play', 'symbolic play' and 'games with rules'. The first refers to the sensorimotor and exploratory play of infants between six months and two years; symbolic play includes fantasy and socio-drama play of children of nursery and infant school age; while games with rules are characteristic in the activities of children from six years onward. To Piaget's scheme Smilanksy (1968) added 'constructive play' to include activities in which objects are manipulated to construct or create something. But as Smith (1990) observes, the forms of play that are characteristic of children's behaviour during school playtime do not fit into these categories, for example, physical activities like running, climbing, swinging and sliding, or rough and tumble play, such as play fighting, wrestling and chasing.

Burns (1986) makes a distinction between pre-social and social play, which provides a useful distinction as it focuses on the socialising aspects of play. *Pre-social play* of early infancy occurs when a young baby plays with inanimate objects like bells, rattles and balls which dangle from its crib – and also when the baby plays with itself, as it explores its face, fingers and toes, and sex organs. This type of pre-social play is *exploratory play*, in it an infant explores its environment. As the infant becomes more mobile so it will crawl around to inspect features in a widening physical life space. The next stage is *parallel play* and this is often the child's first contact with another child.

> Even before an infant is ready to interact with other children, it may choose to play beside them, but not with them. A child may bring a favourite toy to another child's side, then sit and play with the toy (but not the other child) for minutes on end.
>
> (Burns, 1986)

A third type of pre-social play is *instigative play*. Here the child may indulge in 'follow-the-leader' or 'peek-a-boo' play, but the behaviour of another person directly instigates the child's activity. 'Instigative play is the final step, possibly, towards true social interaction' (Burns, 1986). *Social play* develops with age and has more relevance for understanding the value of the play in the primary school and how it can fit into the curriculum. Here play becomes more complex and other people become interactive partners rather than objects to be manipulated. Burns (1986) named three major types of social play – free play, creative play and formal play. Physical *free play* with other children is probably the easiest for a child to engage in and is of critical importance in the socialisation process. Play fighting between peers is common from three years on through to adolescence – especially with boys. Wrestling involves close physical contact in which each child struggles to pin his partner to the ground – in most cases it is not for real and roles are quickly reversed. Chasing play is an extension of rough-and-tumble, and the screams from an infant playground will demonstrate it is exciting and emotionally stimulating. The danger with these kinds of boisterous play is that they can become more serious in intent – especially for the most aggressive child. Later we shall discuss this kind of play in the context of bullying.

> The friendly intent in play of this kind is typically signalled by smiling and laughter. At the preschool age play fighting seems distinct from serious fighting, at least in the great majority of cases. The former is carried out with friends, who often stay together after the episode. The

latter is often not between friends, involves different facial expressions and the participants usually do not stay together after the encounter. Preschool children themselves seem to be aware of the difference. However, there is some evidence that towards adolescence strength and dominance become more important in the choice of partners in play fighting, and the distinction from real aggressive intent is possibly not always so clear.

(Smith and Cowie, 1991)

Creative play is primarily pretend or fantasy play, in which a stick becomes a gun and a blanket a house. The imaginary use of inanimate objects can extend to having an imaginary companion who accompanies the child at mealtimes, in the car, to the shops, and so, on to bed. As many as a third of parents reported their child had some form of imaginary companion (Partington and Grant, 1984). Language is an important part of play, as children develop the 'scripts' associated with role playing, such as mummies and daddies, doctors and nurses, monsters, cops, cowboys and spacemen. The use of language in sociodrama will extend into the rhymes and word games documented by the Opies (1959, 1969) to be discussed in the section on the playground.

Formal play involves cooperation with others in games and activities that are rule-governed. Role playing referred to above will have some rule structure but it is more likely to be particular to that single play episode. More generally applied rules come into operation at the age of six or seven years in games like tag, hopscotch, marbles and football. These are games with public rules to which all participants are expected to conform.

Transition from play to games is a gradual process, as children develop a greater appreciation and respect for the nature of rules. In his influential book *The Moral Judgement of the Child* (1932) Piaget developed his interest in the moral reasoning of children as a consequence of watching them play in a Geneva suburb where he describes boys playing marbles. He was interested in how children acquired the rules of the game, where they thought they came from, and whether they could be changed. From his observations Piaget distinguished three stages in children's awareness of rules:

Stage one: (up to 4–5 years) – rules were not understood
Stage two: (from 5 to 9–10 years) – rules regarded as coming from a higher authority and were absolute
Stage three: (from 10 onwards) – rules were mutually agreed by players so were open to change by common consent.

Play and the curriculum

As the aim of the school curriculum is to cater for the different aspects of child development so we can see how play can be integrated into that process.

(1)   *Social development*
Play involves the child in learning to share and cooperate. He learns to adapt his wishes to the wishes of others, to lead and be led. Play also helps the child to establish warm and friendly relationships with other children and build independence and self-control. All of this helps the child to build his self-concept and even a child with limited physical abilities can gain some prestige and sense of achievement (see the story about Zack the Whack, p.105). Moral learning can be derived from social play as children learn to play to rules and develop qualities of obedience, reliability, self-control, unselfishness and loyalty.

(2)   *Intellectual development*
Play is highly motivated behaviour as it is done for enjoyment, which means that teachers and parents have a strongly educative force on their side. The borderline between what is work and what is play is blurred, and the dichotomy evident in the adult mind vanishes in children's activities such that in early childhood they can be encouraged to develop desirable attitudes to school and school work through the pleasures of play. It is through play that a child begins to learn about shape, textures, colour, capacity and weight. And as he makes things the child learns to make judgements, to compare and contrast. Additionally, play fosters the use of language and curiosity, and encourages each child to use his intellectual powers.

(3)   *Physical development*
Physical play improves children's health and development as it stimulates growth, increases strength and respiratory activity. Physical play is also important for the development of motor and manipulative coordination, body control and self-confidence in the use of equipment and apparatus. Physical education and games lessons contribute to a growing appreciation of the need for rules in all kinds of games. Children enter into organised competitive activities through playing for school teams, although they should not become so competitive that it takes the enjoyment out of playing. In such circumstances the pursuit of trophies can introduce an unhealthy drive for competition and a

concentration on the few who excel to the neglect of the majority of pupils. Play can also provide a 'safety valve' for pent-up feelings and channel aggression into socially acceptable activities.

(4) *Creative aesthetic development*

Play can stimulate the child's imagination through fantasy and pretend activities. The games they play during playtimes can be a constructive and creative extension of the classroom. They enter into rhymes and word games, use the apparatus about the adventure playground and use their imagination as they chase, hide, drive racing cars and so on.

Playtime and the school playground

For both pupils and teachers playtime is an important part of the school day, as both regard it as recreational, non-work time. In fact, it could be said that the school day revolves around the morning and afternoon breaks and the longer lunchtime break. Blatchford (1989) calculated that in his study 28 per cent of the school day is spent in playtime and much of it in the playground. Which, he maintains, was about the same time spent in the total given to mathematics, writing and reading. Yet, considering the amount of time given to it little research has been conducted into playtime and only recently have schools begun to develop a policy on how to constructively use the playground. Considering the importance accorded to play it is particularly surprising that playtime in schools has received so little attention. Blatchford (1989) calls it, 'the forgotten part of the school day'.

Some of the most influential work on children's play has been done by Iona and Peter Opie (1959; 1969). In their publications they describe the seasonal customs, initiation rites, superstitious practices and beliefs, rhymes and chants, catcalls and retorts, jokes, riddles and nicknames, plus innumerable traditional games common in playgrounds throughout Britain. In *Children's Games in Street and Playground* (1969) they describe games in which children hunt and chase, play hide and seek, race each other, compete in trials of skill and strength, play 'dare' and 'who's got the ball?'. Their work groups together over 2,500 named games derived from over 10,000 children attending state schools during the 1960s. Some of the games can be traced back to Elizabethan, medieval and even ancient times. The conclusion they arrive at is that left to their own devices children will play and pass on these colourful and resourceful games, in a world set apart from the control of adults. They are part of children's culture which enables them to gain a measure of control over their own environment.

In a very different kind of study of children's play Sluckin (1981; 1987) chose to carry out an observational investigation of children in a primary school playground. He arrived at three conclusions:

> Firstly, I noticed that there is order amongst the apparent chaos of playground life. You do not have to look very closely to realize that children at playtime are not just like little savages (as some of their teachers describe them). But there is indeed a sense in which playground life can be said to be primitive. My second conclusion was that although the activities or content of the children's world usually differ from those of adults, the means or processes by which children and adults manage their worlds are remarkably similar. According to the Opies (1969), the day-to-day running of playground life involves affidavits, promissory notes, claims, deeds of conveyance, receipts and notices of resignation, all of which are verbal and all sealed by the utterance of ancient words which are recognized and considered binding by the whole community. My third conclusion was that experience in the playground provides an important preparation for adult social life.
>
> (Sluckin, 1987)

Sluckin also noted a playground pecking order – even in the pre-school playground, where there are rules, roles and rituals which pupils must learn if they are to successfully negotiate episodes of potential and actual conflict. Thus, entering the social world of the playground with its coded messages, faces children with social problems of entry and continuity of membership. In his study of conflict resolution he draws attention to the power of ritual words like 'bags' or 'bagsee', which is used by children throughout Britain. 'Bagsee mine' gains possession, 'bagsee me first' claims precedence, and 'bagsee me not it' avoids a role. For the child, bagsee and other similar words, helps get you what you want and, most particularly, redefines the situation in your favour, where there is conflict in fighting or pretend games. Sluckin argues that playground activities serve an important role in children's social development, as they develop strategies

> to resolve all sorts of everyday social problems, such as joining in a game, excluding others, avoiding a role, starting and stopping fights, insulting, threatening, bribing, gaining a reputation and the public and private management of friendships with the opposite sex.
>
> (Sluckin, 1987)

In the apparent chaos of playtime there exists an order and culture which contains elements that are a preparation for adult life, involving cooperation, regulated competition, contracts and a rule system to protect the rights of the weak and constrain the powerful.

> Most important of all is that growing up in the playground offers a setting where children have a high motivation to learn how to get on with their peers. During games they are able to initiate, discuss, influence and change rules in a way that just could not happen between child and adult. Indeed, when teachers supervise play it is all too often precisely these types of opportunities that are missing. It is simply not the case, as one headteacher claimed, that anything a child learns in the playground could equally well be learnt in the classroom. As adults we need to have respect for the self-motivated learning that takes place away from the direct influence of adults and yet provide just those experiences that help prepare for adulthood. As one 5-year-old told me, 'playtime makes me grow up extremely slowly'.
>
> (Sluckin, 1987)

Unfortunately, playtime is not a happy time for some children and Blatchford (1989), as part of a wider, longitudinal study of a sample of children in 33 schools, from their nursery class to the end of their first year in junior school (Tizard *et al.*, 1988), found that two thirds of children interviewed were distressed by teasing and name-calling, and also upset by being provoked into fighting – these latter were mainly boys. In his discussions with teachers, many confirmed this aspect of children's playtime behaviour. In their view there was a good deal of unnecessarily aggressive and anti-social behaviour in the form of squabbling, jumping on backs and kicking, as children acted out scenes from television programmes and video films. Other teachers were particularly concerned about verbal abuse, especially the calling of racist names. In a study of playground behaviour in Northern Ireland, it is suggested by Austin (1986) that the playground is a powerful forum for the socialising of children into cultural identities – in this case the sectarianism of Catholics and Protestants.

Blatchford's work leads directly to the following section on bullying but firstly there is need to consider his observation about the traditional school playground, for he maintains that this impoverished environment actually contributes to behavioural problems. To highlight the lack of stimulation in so many playgrounds one only needs to contrast it with the colourful and exciting corridor and classroom displays in most primary schools. In many schools the 'yard' can be a battlefield as children of different ages compete for space. Many teachers in his study said that they witnessed few traditional games and rhymes, as the dominant games were football and different forms of chasing play. The problem is compounded by a lack of supervision and the provision of inappropriate supervision during the long dinner break. During lunchtime pupils are under the control of mid-day supervisors who, in the majority of cases, are undertrained and underpaid for what is a highly responsible and demanding job. There is a growing number of organisations and publications devoted to making the playground environment a more stimulating and creative place for children (see Ross and Ryan, 1990; Tattum and Lane, 1988; Tattum and Herbert, 1990), and training programmes for mid-day supervisors (OPTIS, 1986). But before we paint too bleak a picture of playtime Blatchford *et al.* (1990) found that the majority of eleven year olds interviewed liked playtimes and the long mid-day break. Their reasons were that they provided relief from work, a time to play games and meet with friends from another class. Another reason children enjoy breaktimes is that there is only minimal adult supervision and they are able to engage in their own 'chosen activities'. This point should not be underestimated in any scheme to improve supervision for, as the Opies and Sluckin point out, it is the impenetrability to adults of children's culture that permits the cultural transmission of games, rhymes and ritual words. And although a number of pupils, more particularly girls, complained about disruptive behaviour in the playground, their main objection was to being forced to go outside even on cold and damp days.

In considering the merits and demerits of playtime for the social and personal development of children there are some issues which need to be considered. Firstly, if playtime is for the recreational benefit of pupils should they be obliged to use the playground when they would prefer to be inside reading or some other activity? One accepts the problem of supervision but that is not insurmountable, and children should also be placed on trust. Secondly, can we permit the rough and tumble, aggressive behaviour of a minority of pupils to spoil the enjoyment of the rest. Furthermore, the rough and competitive aspects of playground culture are in contrast to the kinds of attitudes and behaviours teachers wish to cultivate as part of personal and social education. Thirdly, classroom and playground are not distinct separate places but integrated into a pupil's day. Negative behaviour during playtime will enter the classroom and result in disruptive behaviour and pupil–pupil conflicts. For these and other reasons, school staff need to give more thought to playtime and the playground, to make them constructive parts of the school day.

Bullying in schools

In Chapter 3 we discussed the concept of pupil career and noted that school provides opportunities for pupils to follow both legitimate and illegitimate career paths. In that chapter the careers of disrupter and truant were examined and here we shall consider the *interactive* careers of bullies and bullied.

That there are links between these different anti-social behaviours will be regarded as self-evident by teachers and there is a growing body of research evidence to support this belief. Disruptive pupils and bullies are children who direct their aggression towards different persons, in the former it is against a teacher and in the latter against another pupil. That many bullies are also troublesome in class is supported by O'Moore and Hillery (1991) and Mooij (1991). Similarly children who are victims of bullying may stay away from school for fear of what awaits them. Reid (1989) reported that 15 per cent of persistent absentees in his study gave bullying as the reason why they started on a career of truancy. Knox (1988) also argues that many children who become school phobics are the victims of bullying, although, she quite rightly maintains that these children are really expressing a *rational* fear of the dreadful things that are done to them by other pupils. That we recognise the inter-relationship between these forms of anti-social behaviours is important, as it means that in tackling one our strategies will also positively influence other unwanted behaviour. And in this chapter we will discuss a range of intervention approaches to reduce bullying and these should be read in conjunction with the recommendations to reduce disruptive behaviour and truancy (pp. 67–8 and 73 respectively).

One of the most surprising things about bullying is that we have taken so long to recognise its seriousness and extent. In August 1987 the authors attended the first European Conference on Bullying in Schools, held in Stavanger, Norway. The Scandinavian countries had studied the problem for many years but none of the delegates from the other participating countries could report any significant national interest – and this included the United Kingdom (see O'Moore, 1988). Since then there has been a growing interest in the problem and a number of books and resource materials have been produced. There is also a DES funded research project based at Sheffield University

(Ahmad *et al.*, 1991). In addition to the growth of interest in Britain there have been increased expressions of concern at an international level, to include countries such as USA, Canada, Australia, Japan, Holland and Eire, amongst others (see Roland and Munthe, 1989; Tattum and Tattum, 1992).

It is difficult to understand why the education community in general has taken so long to acknowledge that bullying is a serious problem. For all who have attended schools as pupils and teachers know that it exists – and many people have distressing stories to tell about their own or family's experiences. Can it be that bullying is regarded as an inevitable part of school life, with its initiation ceremonies, boisterous play, gang games and teasing. In fact, Rigby and Slee (1990) suggest that here are features in the school environment that harden the attitudes of children towards victims – maybe its competitive ethos. Adults are also prone to dismiss it with hollow clichés, such as 'boys will be boys', 'they have got to learn to look after themselves' and 'it will prepare them for the real world'. Yet how many adults would tolerate abuse and harassment in their workplace without making a complaint?

Another thought on adult attitudes is contained in the following nonsense rhyme:

> *Tell tale tit, your tongue shall be slit,*
> *And all the doggies in the town shall have a little bit*

Only thoughtless adults could burden a child with such a fearful rule, for such an injunction is a 'bully's charter'. The bully is protected by a misplaced code of secrecy amongst children but this rhyme reinforces it by suggesting that a worse offence is to be a tell-tale, a sneak, or a grass. It is a rule which is kept by confused, vulnerable children who are told by adults to be truthful and honest and are abandoned by those same authorities when they turn to them for help.

(Tattum and Tattum, 1992)

Pupil victims are also reluctant to tell their parents or teachers for fear of making the bullying worse. They are ashamed of what is happening to them, as they often believe that they are the only one singled out for such treatment. This causes them to think that there really is something wrong with them and in extreme cases assume an attitude of self-reproach and guilt. This low perception of self is damaging and can remain with a child into adolescence and adulthood (Tattum and Tattum, 1992).

In their study into the self-concept of 783 children between seven and thirteen years, O'Moore and Hillery (1991) found that children who were victims of bullying had low self-esteem, and saw themselves in negative terms of being troublesome, more anxious, less popular, and less happy and satisfied than children who had never been bullied.

> We believe that in order to effect any real change in bullying behaviour one must tackle the root cause of the problem. From our results we have reason to believe that low self-esteem is a contributory factor in bullying ... Whereas a few successful or unsuccessful experiences may not have a major effect on the self-concept, it is the frequency and consistency of feelings of adequacy or inadequacy over a period of years which leaves its mark on the self-concept.
>
> It has been repeatedly shown that whether or not children come to school with a firm picture of their self-worth, teachers have the potential to employ the academic and social learning experiences of school to either reinforce or reteach children a positive view of themselves.
>
> All too often, however, schools overlook the emotional needs of the child in their efforts to achieve academic results. For example, it is not uncommon to hear teachers express the view that 'due to curricular and examination pressure we have no time to spend on the social and emotional problems of students'. Yet, self-concept contributes positively towards both academic success and social and emotional adjustment.
>
> (O'Moore and Hillery, 1991)

In their study the authors found that bullies too held feelings of low self-worth in relation to intellectual and school status.

What is bullying?

There is need for us to examine what we understand to be bullying behaviour for we have in the past held too narrow and simplistic a view. There is also a belief that because bullying is by its very nature a secretive activity, done away from the eyes of adults, there is little that teachers can do to reduce its occurrence. In fact, a number of studies reflect the under-estimation by teachers of bullying when compared with self and peer reports by pupils.

In this section we shall consider the complexity of the interaction between bully and bullied by looking at its nature, frequency, intensity and motivation. But firstly we turn to the Elton Report (1989) to demonstrate that teachers in that survey were well aware of the behaviour in their classrooms and about the school. (Background details to the survey and Report can be found on pp. 65–7. Table 5 combines data extracted from the Report (Tables 1, 2, 9 and 10) which deal specifically with bullying.

Table 5: The Elton Report: Sheffield University Survey (October, 1988)

Bullying behaviour observed at least once during the survey week by:

PRIMARY TEACHERS (n = 1,200)

	In class	About school
Physical assaults: pushing, punching, striking	74%	86%
Verbal abuse: offensive/insulting remarks	55%	71%
SECONDARY TEACHERS (n = 3,200)		
Physical assaults:	42%	66%
Verbal abuse:	62%	76%

The nature of bullying

There are a number of definitions of bullying and the following by Roland is comprehensive:

> Bullying is longstanding violence, physical or psychological, conducted by an individual or a group and directed against an individual who is not able to defend himself in the actual situation.
>
> (Roland, 1988)

In addition we offer a very short definition because it enables us to emphasise two particular factors in bully–victim interaction.

> Bullying is a wilful, conscious desire to hurt another and put him/her under stress.
>
> (Tattum, 1988)

We offer the above short definition because it focuses on two important aspects of the interactive nature of bullying. Firstly, it draws attention to the fact that bullies know what they are doing and that it is wrong. In our view an accidental or unwitting, hurtful action would not constitute bullying – with one proviso, unless it was perceived to be so by the victim. Bullies get satisfaction from holding power over another less aggressive and vulnerable person. From the victim's point of view, stress is created not only by what actually happens but by the threat and fear of what may happen. The bully does not have to be physically present for a child to be anxious and distressed – he may not sleep or want to go to school, suffer tummy upsets or headaches, peer around corners or not use the school toilets for fear of meeting the bully or bullies.

Bullying can be of a physical or verbal nature, but it can also take the form of other psychologically damaging behaviour such as intimidation, extortion, exclusion, spreading of malicious rumours and threatening gestures. Physical bullying can range in severity from a punch to an assault with a dangerous weapon, as in the case of Ahmed Ullah, a thirteen year old Asian boy, who was murdered in the playground of Burnage High School in 1986. (A report on the Inquiry by Ian MacDonald Q.C. can be found in MacDonald *et al.*, 1989.) Verbal abuse can also range from teasing and taunting to abusive comments about a person's appearance, which can be emotionally bruising. In fact, the rhyme below is misleading and untrue:

Sticks and stones may break my bones,
But names will never hurt me.

Racial and sexual harassment are particularly insidious forms of bullying, as they attack the most fundamental characteristics of a person's being – their sense of self. In his study of the primary school playground Blatchford (1989) expresses concern about racism during playtimes, and not only the behaviour of children, which often reflects parental prejudices, but also the attitudes of mid-day supervisors. Unfortunately, teachers can also give support to racist attitudes by the things they say and do (Kelly and Cohn, 1988). The following examples are taken from the Commission for Racial Equality's report *Learning in Terror* (1988):

> The decision was taken to leave the district by a couple in a small country town in the Home Counties. The mother is German and the father Cypriot. Their 13 year old daughter was subjected to a strange combination of epithets: 'Nazi' in relation to her mother and 'Wog' and 'Paki' in relation to her father. The child and her mother had also been attacked in their home by stone-throwing youngsters from the school. The school response was poor, and the police advised the family to move away.
>
> (Case B)
>
> At a primary school in the North-West a black child was forced by the teacher to stand up and spell out the word 'golliwog' when the child refused to read it out in class because he found it offensive.
>
> (Case D)

A young Sikh published his own account of the regular verbal and physical harassment that he had experienced in the seven years he had spent at schools in the South. Much of that harassment was directed at his hair and turban, both regarded as sacred symbols. Sometimes teachers would join in or even initiate the jokes. The main effect, he said, was to erode his self-confidence and capacity to concentrate on learning.

(Case J)

The numbers involved in bullying

Having discussed the nature of bullying it is important that we accept that it is widespread and persistent, and to be found in *all* our schools and colleges. Including nursery class, infant, junior and secondary schools, special schools, and in both state and independent sectors.

The most comprehensive survey into the incidence of bullying was carried out in Norway in 1983. It was a nationwide survey funded by the Ministry of Education and involved some 140,000 junior and senior high school pupils – eight to sixteen year olds. The results of a self-report questionnaire indicated that approximately 15 per cent of children were involved – 9–10 per cent victims and 5–6 per cent bullies. If we convert this percentage to state schools in the UK, where we have a school population of about 8.6 million, then the disturbing figure of around 1.3 million pupils are involved. In the independent sector 15 per cent would represent some 87,000 children and young people. But the growing body of research in the UK, mainly small-scale, local studies, indicates that a higher proportion of pupils are involved in our schools. Of interest to primary schools is the work of Stephenson and Smith (1988). In their 1982 survey in 26 schools in Cleveland they collected data from 49 teachers on 1,078 final year primary school children. Teachers indicated that 23 per cent of their children were involved in bullying – 7 per cent victims, 10 per cent bullies and 6 per cent in the dual role of bully and victim. In a later study of 143 children in the top two year groups in one primary school the researchers found a 'high level of agreement between nominations made by teacher and children in the study as to which children were involved in bullying (Correlation = 0.8)'. Similar high levels of agreement was also found by Olweus (1978). These disturbingly high figures, which suggest that in excess of one in five primary school children are involved in bullying behaviour are supported by Ahmad and Smith (1989), who administered a self-report questionnaire similar to the Norwegian instrument to about 2,000 pupils in seven middle schools and four secondary schools in the South Yorkshire area. In response to questions on frequency of being bullied 17 per cent said they had been moderately bullied (sometimes/now and then) and severely bullied (once a week). Using a similar categorisation of frequency 6 per cent admitted they had bullied other children. These high figures are supported in a study of two secondary schools (234 pupils) by Yates and Smith (1989), in which the figures, using the same categories given above, were 20 per cent victims and 6 per cent bullies.

On considering some of the data from other countries there is evidence of figures comparable with those in England. In a study in Toronto, Canada, of 211 students from 14 classes (grades 4 to 8) it was found that 20 per cent were bullied 'now and then' and 'weekly or more often' (Ziegler and Rosenstein-Manner, 1991). An interesting feature of this project is that the researchers also asked the children's parents and teachers about whether they were aware of how often children in the school were bullied. In both cases there was an underestimation compared with the students' experiences. Fourteen per cent of parents were aware that their child had been bullied 'now and then' or 'weekly or more often'; and when their teachers were asked, 'How many students in your class have been bullied at least once a week in school this term?', as many as 14 per cent replied zero (compared with 6 per cent students) and 7 per cent just 'Didn't know'.

Once again using a self-report questionnaire Rigby and Slee (1990) surveyed 676 pupils in three primary schools and one high school in Adelaide, Australia, and found that when they pooled the responses to the question asking, 'How often have you been bullied?', for the categories 'pretty often' and 'very often' the figures were 17 per cent for boys and 11 per cent for girls.

Before leaving this section on the extent of the problem a cautionary word is provided by Mellor (1990), whose survey of 942 pupils in ten secondary schools in Scotland found incidences of 6 per cent who were bullied 'sometimes or more often' and 4 per cent who bullied 'sometimes or more often'.

Regardless of which figures we accept the proportions of children involved are far too high for any complacency. They must be a concern for all who work with children, as the numbers represent a very large number of unhappy children in our schools, both victims and bullies, who need help from teachers, parents and other professional groups.

Frequency and duration is also a factor to be considered and we do not regard isolated incidents, however severe, as bullying. In cases we have encountered when counselling families, the victim has suffered for weeks, months and years. Furthermore, bullying gangs can terrorise a playground. It is probably the case that gang bullying can be more unpleasant and harmful to the victim. Stephenson and Smith (1988) found that 41 per cent of bullies said that they encouraged other children to join with them in bullying. The message is that where there is a bullying gang no-one is safe. In Tattum and Herbert (1990) a distinction is made between children who are 'supporters' or 'spectators' and at this level teachers need to challenge children in their classes to consider their position – for if they are not part of the solution then they are part of the problem!

In their bullying, boys are more likely to inflict physical assaults whilst girls tend to use the more psychological methods, such as name-calling and exclusion from the group. Bullies are also overly aggressive and destructive, and they enjoy dominating other children so that they quickly misinterpret an innocent bump or careless intrusion as an attack or insult. In other words, their victims may be any unfortunate who crosses their path, so that the traditional stereotype of a victim as someone who is overtly different in their appearance or behaviour over-simplifies the complex nature of bully–victim interaction.

The traditional view that wearing glasses, having red hair, fatness and so on, does not necessarily apply. In fact, they are often post-facto adult rationalisations. Generally speaking, however, victims tend to be physically weaker than other boys whilst bullies are stronger and bigger than average (Olweus, 1984). In an attempt to extend our understanding of the problem Stephenson and Smith (1988) distinguish between bullies and anxious bullies, and victims and provocative victims. It is also incorrect to assume that children are either one or the other, for some bullies are also victims. O'Moore and Hillery (1991) found that children who were both bullies and victims in different social contexts had more unhealthy psychological qualities than children who filled a single role of bully or victim.

Finally, in this section on the incidence of bullying, it is important to note that a number of studies report a decline in frequency as children get older. This feature is indicated in Fig. 13 from the Norwegian survey (Olweus, 1988). This pattern is also supported by Ziegler and Rosenstein-Manner (1991) in their Canadian study, as shown in Table 6.

We may in part explain these figures by recognising that young children of infant and lower junior age are more prepared to talk about their problems and turn to adults (not peers) for help and

152

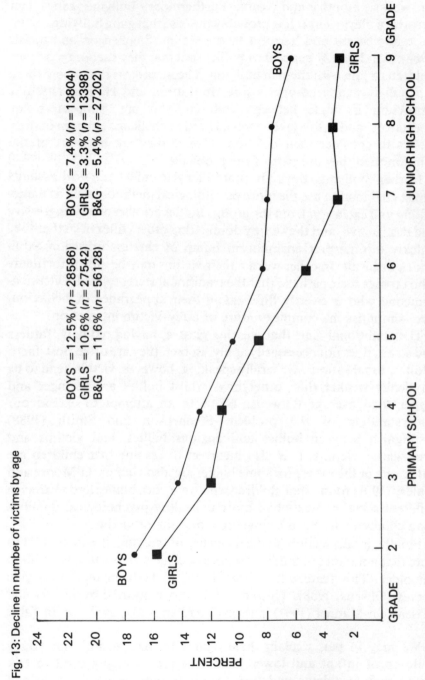

Fig. 13: Decline in number of victims by age

BOYS = 12.5% (n = 28586)
GIRLS = 10.6% (n = 27542)
B&G = 11.6% (n = 56128)

BOYS = 7.4% (n = 13804)
GIRLS = 3.3% (n = 13398)
B&G = 5.4% (n = 27202)

Source: Olweus, 1988.

Table 6: Age of victims of bullying

Age in years	Percentage who are victims n = 43
9	40%
10	30%
11	21%
12	30%
13	8%
14	5%

support. No doubt it is also the case that they are more often bullied in the playground than older pupils simply because as pupils move up the school there are few bigger and older children to abuse you. It is because young children are more at risk that we should be particularly vigilant in the infant school. In a new project (September, 1991) Roland (1991) has decided to direct his three year Sandness Project at working to influence the attitudes and behaviour of Grade I (seven and eight year olds) pupils in 9 schools, involving 20 classes and about 400 children. This action is an extension of his Janus Project (1989a,b) and is based on the slogan 'A Good Start in the First Class' – a sentiment all schools would do well to adopt on the issue of bullying, as starting in junior or secondary school can be too late. The aims of the project are to establish good interpersonal relationships and behaviour patterns in the first class, which will extend into the rest of the school as the children get older and also, to encourage teachers to analyse and share their accumulated knowledge and coping strategies with colleagues in their own school and the other project schools.

Another group at risk are new pupils to a school, including the cohort of children who transfer from primary to secondary school. From being senior pupils in the primary school they become the youngest and most vulnerable group in the comprehensive. Not only are they the targets of seniors (especially second and third formers) but also pupils from different feeder primaries, as they work out the new playground 'pecking order'. From the reported anxieties of pupils about the transfer bullying is one of their most prominent worries (see Fig. 4, p. 61). In an effort to prevent bully–victim interactive careers from developing secondary schools should work with their feeder primaries as part of a joint anti-bullying policy. Actions could include:

(1) That primary schools should give to the secondary schools the names of children who are likely targets of bullying. Form tutors

should then watch for any changes in behaviour and work, and consider nominating someone to either openly befriend that child or watch at a distance as a 'secret friend'. The latter scheme can also work well in helping new individual pupils settle in a school at any time during the academic year.

(2) The new cohort should use a designated part of the playground away from their predatory seniors – this scheme may only last for a term. It is recognised that the playground is the most common location for bullying.

(3) Each primary school could invite pupils from the previous year's cohort to talk to the year six pupils to allay their fears and answer their questions.

(4) The secondary school should ensure that every first year is placed in a class with at least one friend from the primary. Research (see p.130) indicates that this simple exercise reduces anti-social behaviour and encourages favourable attitudes towards the feelings of others.

Bullying and peer relationships

In this chapter on social education and peer relationships it is important that we examine how bullies and victims are regarded by other pupils. Their perceptions are vitally important for any anti-bullying programme a school may organise which seeks to involve *all* children. By creating the right kind of ethos in which one child does not try to dominate another we can encourage pupils to intervene in bullying activities when adults are not around – in the playground and to and from school.

In their recent research involving 211 students age nine to fifteen years in Toronto schools, Ziegler and Rosenstein-Manner (1991) asked the children how they personally respond to bullying. From the data in

Table 7: Children's response to bullying

What I do	
Nothing; not my business	24%
Nothing; but I should	33%
I try to help	42%
What I feel	
I don't feel much	10%
It's somewhat unpleasant	29%
It's very unpleasant	61%

Table 7 most children feel distressed by bullying and are willing, although not always able, to help. Ten per cent said they were indifferent to other children's distress but the majority (75 per cent) felt that they should help the victim.

These encouraging findings are supported by Rigby and Slee (1990) who produced a pro-victim scale with three factors to look at the attitudes of children towards the victims of bullying (see Table 8).

Table 8: Selected items from the Provictim Scale with percentage responses

Item Content	Responses (Percentages)		
	Agree	Unsure	Disagree
Support for victims			
1. I like it when somebody stands up for kids who get kids who get bullied	82.0	13.2	4.8
2. It's a good thing to help children who can't defend themselves.	63.3	26.3	10.5
3. It makes me angry when a kid gets picked on without reason.	81.9	14.0	4.1

The result demonstrates a basic sense of decency by the majority of pupils as they give positive responses to 'Support for Victims' and express their disapproval of bullying behaviour. There is clearly a great deal of good will on which teachers can draw in class discussions about bullying and schools can use to support any intervention strategies they may implement.

Intervention strategies

Bullying is a form of behaviour which damages interpersonal relation-ships and can result in long-term, adverse effects for both bully and victim (Tattum and Tattum, 1992). To reduce these destructive effects on a school's ethos there must be a whole-school approach. As it is a secretive activity we need strategies which aim to change attitudes towards bullying and establish a climate which will not tolerate one member oppressing another. Each school must heighten the awareness of teaching and non-teaching staff so that they are more alert to the extent of bullying and its harmful effects. This may require a survey to convince some teachers of its prevalence and frequency in their school (Ahmad and Smith, 1990).

At the centre of its whole-school approach a school must have a policy on how it may be tackled and reduced. To this end a policy statement must be drawn up and communicated to all parents and pupils. The

156

Governing Body should be involved in its preparation and reiteration, as the 1986 and 1988 Education Act charge them with legal responsibility for the conduct of the school and discipline. The Advisory Centre for Education (ACE, 1990) has produced an invaluable information sheet on 'Governors and Bullying'.

(Tattum and Tattum, 1992)

Reasons why a school needs a whole-school policy and sets of procedures are listed below; a more detailed discussion of each can be found in Tattum and Tattum (1992).

Reasons for a whole-school policy

(1) To counter the view that bullying is an inevitable part of school life.
(2) To move beyond a crisis-management approach to a more preventative ethos.
(3) To open up discussion at all levels from a full staff development day to class/tutorial groups.
(4) To involve more people in the identification and condemnation of bullying.
(5) To draw up an agreed set of procedures for staff to follow when inquiring into a case of bullying.
(6) To create a supportive climate and break down the code of secrecy.
(7) To provide a safe, secure learning environment for all pupils – for this is the right of every child and young person attending our schools.

In Tattum and Tattum (1992) we discuss the following five elements of a whole-school anti-bullying programme but here we shall only discuss in detail items two and five on the school community and the curriculum.

Elements of whole-school approach

(1) A policy statement declaring the unacceptability of bullying.
(2) A multi-level approach involving a wide range of people – the school community.
(3) Both long-term and short-term strategies. These are dealt with in the section on the Norwegian Campaign (p. 160).

(4) A wide discussion of bullying to open up the issues and tackle what is a complexed problem.

(5) An anti-bullying campaign needs to be integrated within the school curriculum.

The school community (Item 2 above)

It is important that teaching and non-teaching staff are involved in the discussion and implementation of an anti-bullying programme. Most bullying takes place about the school grounds – in the playground, toilets, dinner queues and in a variety of other locations. It takes place during school hours at times when pupils are less closely supervised. Therefore, to counter the secretive element of bullying every school should use the large number of employees who are not teachers.

Fig. 14: Spheres of involvement

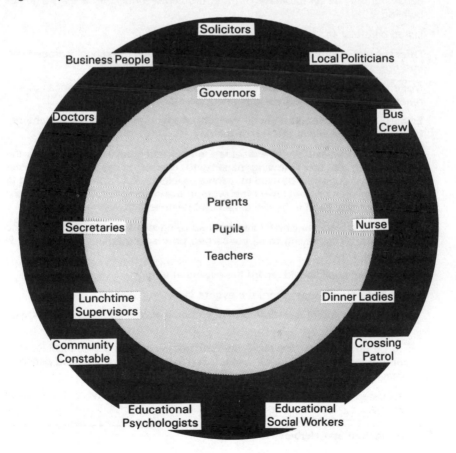

Fig. 14 'Spheres of Involvement' illustrates the wide range of people who can work with the school as part of its whole-school (even community) approach to bullying. Specific advice for parents and governors can be found in Tattum and Herbert (1990) and a list of procedures for teachers is given in Table 9. Senior pupils are particular members of the pupil body who can be used to discourage bullying. They should be talked to about their own attitudes and behaviour as they use or misuse their authority or position in the school. Secretaries, nursery nurses, dinner ladies and lunchtime supervisors can be positively used to discourage bullying. Lunchtime supervisors operate

Table 9: Advice and guidance for teachers

Watch for early signs of distress in pupils – deterioration of work, spurious illness, isolation, the desire to remain with adults, erratic attendance. Whilst this behaviour may be symptomatic of other problems, it may be the early signs of bullying.

Listen carefully and record all incidents.

Offer the victim immediate support and help by putting the school's procedures into operation.

Make the unacceptable nature of the behaviour, and the consequences of any repetition, clear to the bully and his/her parents.

Ensure that all accessible areas of the school are patrolled at break, lunchtime, between lessons and at the end of the day.

Use all the pupils as a positive resource in countering bullying and discuss the advice given on the following page with classes or tutorial group. Peer counselling groups may be used to resolve problems. Pupils can also be used to help shy children or newcomers feel welcome and accepted. Sexual and racial harassment also need to be discussed and dealt with.

The following steps may be followed in recording incidents of bullying and also as a means of conveying to all concerned how seriously the school regards bullying behaviour.

The bullied pupil should record the events *in writing*.

The bully should also record the events *in writing*.

The teacher and/or a senior colleague should record their discussions with both parties.

The parents/carers of the pupils involved should be sent copies of all reports, and the reports placed in the respective pupils' files for a *specified* period of time.

The parents/carers of the pupils should be asked to respond to the above *in writing*.

Source: Tattum and Herbert (1990).

in the heat of the playground action where it is often difficult to distinguish between real fear and pretend in fantasy games or fighting. Schools often expect too much of untrained supervisors and there is a strong case for developing some in-house training for them.

The outside circle represents a very wide range of people who, at different times, may be involved in cases of bullying. Bus crews and Crossing Persons can help a school identify bullies and bullying gangs as they have close witness of pupil behaviour to and from school. The police, doctors and solicitors are increasingly being brought in by families to handle the more extreme cases of physical and verbal bullying. Educational psychologists meet with individual cases but more and more look to have a positive and active role in working with a school on its anti-bullying programme. Finally, an important group of professionals are the Educational Social Workers or Education Welfare Officers who meet the problem at the interface between the home and the school. Of all the forms of anti-social behaviour bullying is the one which can bring parents and teachers into confrontation about the interpretation and response to the problem.

The school curriculum

If we are to tackle bullying behaviour at a school-wide level then it is not sufficient to only focus on occasional lessons in a PSE programme. Neither can it be left to occasional exhortations in morning assembly. The curriculum, both formal and informal, is a vehicle for influencing pupils' perceptions, attitudes and values. Therefore we must use it in a planned way within a whole-school response to the problem of bullying.

A curriculum approach could be tackled through a single subject or developed as part of a cross-curricular programme (Herbert, 1988). If one was to adopt a single subject, for example English, then the approach could be initiated through the reading of an appropriate children's book – Tattum and Herbert (1990) provide extensive lists appropriate for both primary and secondary aged pupils. For the primary school, *The Diddakoi* by Rumer Godden, provides abundant opportunities to discuss bullying through what happens to a young girl, Kizzy, who is half gypsy.

From this starting point a curriculum development plan could extend the work into Maths, in the form of a school survey, and Design Technology, by identifying 'no-go' places in the school and its surrounding play areas. The work could be extended into Drama, Art,

History, RE and PE, in fact, the range is only limited by the National Curriculum. In the videos and workpacks developed by Tattum and Herbert (1992) a curriculum approach is presented along the lines described in this section.

Of the cross-curricular themes identified by the National Curriculum Council the document *Education for Citizenship* (NCC, 1990) provides an excellent format of ideas to deal with knowledge, skills, attitudes and values – and much of the content could easily be used to focus on bullying.

The most comprehensive intervention programme was carried out in Norway in 1983 as part of a national campaign against bullying (Olweus, 1988; Roland, 1991). The main components of the campaign, which was aimed at teachers, parents and pupils, were:

(1)   A 32-page booklet, describing bullying and offering strategies to reduce it, was distributed free of charge to all comprehensive schools in Norway.

(2)   A 4-page leaflet, with information and advice, was distributed to all families with children of school age.

(3)   A 25-minute video cassette depicting bullying incidents.

(4)   A short inventory of questions to provide a baseline measure of nature and incidents of bullying problems and teachers' willingness to intervene.

In summarising the results of the campaign Olweus (1988) optimistically writes, '... the basic message of our findings is clear: It is definitely possible to reduce substantially bully/victim problems in school and related problem behaviours with a suitable intervention program.'

In brief the outcomes were:

A 50% decrease in bully/victim problems during the two years following the campaign, for both boys and girls.

There was no transfer of problems from school to the journey to and from school.

There was also a reduction in general anti-social behaviour such as vandalism, theft and truancy.

There was an increase in pupil satisfaction with school life, especially reflected in an enjoyment of playtimes.

(Olweus, 1988)

These encouraging results are supported by a follow-up research programme in Rogaland, the south-west region of Norway, where the

Janus programme was monitored by Roland (1991). After three years intervention, along the lines described above, there was a comparable decline in reported bullying but only in the schools which sustained the programme over the three year period. In schools which were half-hearted or intermittent in delivering and emphasising the programme there was an actual increase in reported incidents (Roland, 1991). As with all attitude and behaviour changing initiatives the clear message is that they must be sustained and reiterated throughout every school year.

Exercises

(1) Systematically observe young children at free play in the playground and at more structured play situations to note the number and types of social interactions that take place.

(2) Ask the children in your class to name three children they would choose to play with and three they would choose to work with. Note the degree of overlap and discuss the choices with the children.

(3) Discuss ways of making your school playground more attractive, interesting and stimulating for all children, taking into account age, sex and interests.

(4) Consider ways whereby teachers and parents can encourage their pupils/children to engage in mutually cooperative activities which will help the development of close friendships.

(5) Conduct a simple survey in your class or school to find out the degree of agreement there is between teachers and pupils over the extent of bullying and which children are bullies or victims.

(6) Introduce a project on bullying to raise staff (teaching and non-teaching) and pupil awareness. Make it a cross-curricular project involving as many classes as possible.

Additional reading

Moyles, J. R. (1989) *Just playing*, OU Press, Milton Keynes, for an excellent overview of play from an educational perspective.

Blatchford, P. (1989) *Playtime in the Primary School*, NFER-Nelson, Windsor. Chapters 3 and 5 deal with improving children's behaviour and the playground environment.

Ross, C. and Ryan, A. (1990) *Can I stay in today Miss?*, Trentham Books, Stoke-on-Trent, offers numerous examples on how to improve the school playground.

162

Herbert, G. (1988) in *Bullying in Schools*, D.P. Tattum and D. A. Lane, discusses a whole-curriculum approach to bullying.

Smith, D. and Stephenson, P. (1991) in *Bullying: A practical guide to coping for schools*, M. Elliot has a section on 'How to Discourage Bullying', and Besag (1989) provides a comprehensive section on 'What to do about bullying'.

PART THREE

A Curriculum Approach

CHAPTER 7

PSD: Curriculum and Community

Introduction

The central concept of this book is that the *self is social*, that is, we become the kind of persons we are from the developmental process of interacting with other people. From being in the company of others we discover ourselves as we cooperate and compete, negotiate and empathise in our daily interpersonal relationships. Also, the social contexts in which we interact are important as they contain overt and covert messages which we interpret and internalise. In this process of *becoming a person*, home and school are the first two most influential socialising contexts in the lives of young children, and in the previous six chapters these agencies have been examined with particular reference to the structural, organisational and interpersonal experiences provided by primary schools. We have developed our analysis of the primary school as a socialising organisation for two reasons: firstly, because social education and personal development is regarded as an inherent part of the daily lives of children in schools and, secondly, because we are firmly of the belief that unless the social climate of the classroom or school is conducive then social education will be sterile, as the process and the product will not be in harmony. We cannot expect children to believe in exhortations to be fair, considerate and helpful if teachers do not display these and other qualities in their relationships with the children and each other.

It is frequently said that *how* one learns is as important as *what* one learns. In the case of social and personal education the how is the moral and social climate that creates positive opportunities for social learning experiences. As teachers we must demonstrate our respect for children as persons and not dismiss them by the things we say or do. Children have fragile self-concepts, which need to be built up by positive messages of regard. We also need to listen to what they have to say and show respect for their views – even if we do not agree with them. Teachers need to display sensitivity as they enter a child's body space, personal possessions and private lives. These and many other instances carry messages which children observe and judge. Teaching is the most visible profession of all – everyone spends many years watching teachers. But children assess teachers' personal qualities as well as their professional skills. In their daily interactions with children teachers must be prepared to admit that they have made a mistake and not be concerned about loss of face; they must also keep their word if a promise has been made to an individual or the class; and, constantly, they must try to see things from the child's point of view.

The social curriculum

In social and personal education, more than in any other aspect of the school curriculum, there needs to be a unity of purpose to which all teachers subscribe and work towards. Unity will be evident as social education is seen as a cohesive and coherent whole running from five to eleven years of age, so that there is no unprofitable repetition but that there is progression. This is a tall order, because the social curriculum is so diffuse and pervasive, more than other parts of the National Curriculum. For this reason it cannot be left to *ad hoc* teaching but must be the responsibility of a senior member of staff to oversee its development throughout the primary school. In some respects a curriculum audit for social education and personal development is very different from an audit of other subjects, as it must start from a fundamental questioning of what kinds of young persons and adults we would wish our children to grow up to be. Questions as basic as this examine the values, beliefs and attitudes teachers as citizens cherish and wish to inculcate in young members of society. This kind of audit unfolds the layers of values which pervade a school's structures, organisation and relationships.

> PSE, therefore, should not be confused with a subject, a slot on the timetable, a particular curriculum innovation. Rather is it about the development of the person – an aim which is as broad as the educational enterprise itself. PSE requires a particular vision of personal growth, rooted in a concept of person that needs to be examined and justified. It requires a close examination of the experience which children receive in all areas of school life and of the ways in which teaching, curriculum content, and relationships shape that experience.
>
> (Pring, 1988)

Having regard for Pring's point that PSE is more than a single subject we believe that it still needs to be given structure and offer the following three elements to assist in understanding and organising the social curriculum.

(1)   The *hidden social curriculum* has been dealt with in detail in the previous six chapters and, as already noted, it creates the social context and social relationships in which the social curriculum is delivered. But as a framework it is also an integral part of the social curriculum.

(2)   The *formal social curriculum* includes those parts of the National Curriculum which schools are required by law to teach. The Education Reform Act 1988 specifies that a balanced and broadly based curriculum should be provided by schools which:

> promotes the spiritual, moral, cultural, mental and physical development of pupils at the school and of society; and prepares such pupils for the opportunities, responsibilities and experiences of adult life.

The omission of 'social development' is surprising although it may be thought to be subsumed under the five other areas of personal development – an assumption which has its dangers as the third element will indicate.

(3)   We have called the third element the *implicit social curriculum*. It is different from the other two elements, as it is represented by the taken-for-granted aspects of primary schools to which teachers invariably refer whenever social education is discussed. It is implicit in the notion of 'the caring school' or the phrase, 'primary schools are warm and friendly places'. They are catch-all phrases which need to be tested against the quality of the social curriculum provided.

For obvious reasons this chapter will concentrate on the 'formal' and 'implicit' social curricula.

The formal social curriculum

The National Curriculum is described in terms of subjects which form the starting point for curriculum planning. The compulsory *core subjects* are English, Mathematics and Science, and other *foundation subjects* are Design and Technology, History, Geography, Music, Art and PE. Religious education is also a special case within the National

Curriculum. Detailed *programmes of study* for each subject set out what is to be taught in each of the four key stages of compulsory schooling. To assess progress in each subject *attainment targets* set out the knowledge, understanding and skills expected of children of different ages and abilities. In most subjects the targets are divided into ten levels and at each level there are precise descriptions of what pupils are expected to know or do. It is evident that most if not all the core and foundation subjects provide opportunities for the development of pupils' social understanding and personal qualities and skills.

Thus, what we have is a highly structured curriculum programme which aims to present a clear framework to secure curriculum continuity at various levels of pupil progress. The danger with such a programme is that cross-curricular work in personal and social education will be lost if teachers retreat into subject specialisms.

The theme developed in this chapter is that the formal curriculum is not the whole curriculum. This sentiment is reiterated time and again by the National Curriculum Council (NCC):

> The whole curriculum of a school, of course, goes far beyond the formal timetable. It involves a range of policies and practices to promote the personal and social development of pupils, to accommodate different teaching and learning styles, to develop positive attitudes and values and to forge an effective partnership with parents and the local community.
>
> (NCC, Circular No. 6, 1989)

Beyond the National Curriculum plus the 'hidden social curriculum', the National Curriculum Council presents personal and social development as a *cross curricular dimension*, which 'cannot be left to chance but needs to be coordinated as an explicit part of a school's whole curriculum policy, both inside and outside the formal timetable' (NCC, Circular No. 6, 1989). Other major cross curricular dimensions which promote social and personal development include equal opportunities for all pupils, irrespective of gender, ability or cultural and ethnic background and also, education for life in a culturally diverse society.

Finally, schools will also need to consider how their provision for pupils accommodates the following five *cross curricular themes*:

● economic and industrial understanding;
● careers education and guidance;
● environmental education;
● health education;
● citizenship.

Fig. 15: A cross-curricular map for personal and social development

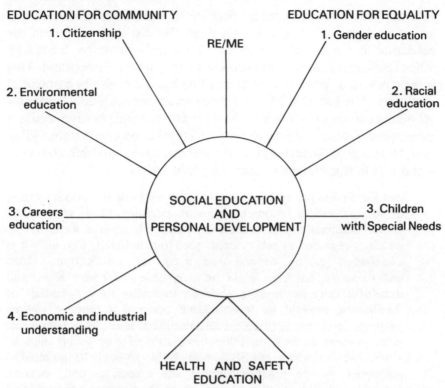

EDUCATION FOR COMMUNITY
1. Citizenship

RE/ME

EDUCATION FOR EQUALITY
1. Gender education

2. Environmental education

2. Racial education

SOCIAL EDUCATION AND PERSONAL DEVELOPMENT

3. Careers education

3. Children with Special Needs

4. Economic and industrial understanding

HEALTH AND SAFETY EDUCATION

From the above breakdown of curriculum provision in the primary school, it will be abundantly evident that social education *for* personal development is complexed and requires a coherent, integrated curriculum development plan if it is to rise above the level of delivery apparent in so many schools. There is need for a senior teacher to take responsibility for its development, otherwise it will continue to be presented in a haphazard and ill-defined way. It is a challenging managerial job with its cross-school role and function. That person must have the status and authority to ask for curriculum information and give firm guidance about the mapping of provision across the age and ability ranges. In Fig. 15 a diagrammatic presentation is given of the way in which a school's curriculum coordinator may begin to develop a structure for personal and social education curriculum. Core and foundation subjects are not included as they already provide the parameters of what *must* be taught as legal requirements of the National Curriculum.

The implicit social curriculum

Primary school teachers accept that social and personal education is an integral part of their role. To them the distinction between the academic and pastoral curriculum, frequently made by secondary school colleagues, is false and something they do not understand. This is the strength of primary school teaching but it can also be a potential weakness. The fact that PSE is viewed as an implicit part of primary schooling can result in it being taken for granted and not discussed in a developmental and systematic way. As a teacher on a staff training day said, 'It is one of those things we do without having to think about it!' – and it is in that statement that the problem lies.

> But therein lies the problem, for what is seen to be self-evidently true, or what is seen to be obviously worth pursuing, rarely receives the critical examination and scrutiny that perhaps it requires. Rarely is that which is regarded as self-evident, spelt out in detail. Certainly it is understood to be beyond the need for justification. Thus, unfortunately, anything might be acceptable under such bland and unhelpful titles as 'helping children to realise their potential' or 'facilitating growth' or 'encouraging personal autonomy'. When personal development (unlike mathematical or scientific development) is 'everywhere' in the school, then there is a need to be doubly cautious – first, because, whatever PSE is, it might just as easily be inhibited as promoted by the practices within the school; second, because something so all-pervasive may be denied the systematic thought and planning that it deserves.
>
> (Pring, 1988)

This inconsistency between what primary school teachers believe happens in their schools and practice was found by Lang (1988b). In his study he discovered that amongst primary and middle school teachers there was a clear desire to acquire the appropriate skills required for effective personal and social development but also found that there was a widespread feeling that PSE was already satisfactorily catered for.

> One significant aspect of the conventional wisdom expressed in a number of the questionnaires was the power attributed to the often very simplistic notion of the 'caring school' ethos – some heads in particular seemed confident that this ethos would satisfactorily meet all pastoral and personal and social needs ... The frequency with which the statement 'this is a very caring school' or its equivalent has been made to me and the occasions where practice did not seem to support

this belief fully leads me to suggest that this may need to be interpreted as a case of (pastoral) incantation.

(Lang, 1988b)

The existence of positive attitudes towards personal and social education amongst primary school teachers at least provides a healthy ethos for the introduction of a more structured curriculum programme. But it is important that teachers also appreciate the power of the 'hidden' social processes that operate in every school. For without understanding and structure the delivery of a complexed PSE curriculum will continue as no more than an act of faith without substance.

Social curriculum and community

One of the great strengths of primary schools is their physical and social closeness to the community. A primary school serves a catchment area which reflects its internal social environment and so provides it with a natural resource. In this section we shall look at both the school as a community and how the school community interacts with its wider, immediate community. What is offered are a number of personal experiences which illustrate both concepts in a very practical way. It is difficult to convey a social climate when faced with a blank page – it has to be observed and experienced. Therefore, to convey the authors' philosophy in practice we shall present a selection of illustrative accounts from the experience of being responsible for the social and personal development of primary age children.

George the Lollipop Man

George the Lollipop Man was a pensioner, he had lived in the village all his life, he knew the children, their parents and grandparents. One wintry morning he slipped on the frosty pavement and was taken to hospital, the fall had badly shaken him and because of his age he was kept under observation for a week. The children dearly missed him and complained that the policeman who had temporarily taken over George's job didn't talk to them as he didn't know their names. So I said, 'Why don't you write to George and tell him how much you miss him?'. Pens were put to paper, letters and cards were written and poems produced. George returned to duty and was profuse in his thanks for the get well wishes and letters.

Two months later a competition appeared in the TV Times to find the 'Lollipop Person of the Year'. The school decided to nominate George and a project was organised involving every class from reception to fourth formers. The letters and cards were produced again by George (who was thrilled and honoured by his nomination) and put into a special folder. More stories, poems, paintings and drawings were collected and a song composed by one pupil – an appreciation of George in words and music on tape. Eventually a large parcel was posted to the competition address before the closing date. Three weeks later the school received a letter from the organisers informing us that from several hundred nominations George had been selected as one of six finalists and an invitation to present himself for an interview in London on a certain date in June was enclosed; travel and hotel expenses would be paid for the finalists. When George came into school that day for his usual cup of tea after his early morning duty he was quite overcome on hearing the news. The Head invited him to attend our morning assembly next day (the timing of assembly was re-arranged to make this possible) so that the whole school could share the good news. In the assembly George thanked the children for all their efforts and kindness and said it was only because of their concern that he would be on his way to London.

Staff and Head discussed ways in which we could give George a good 'send off', it was also suggested that money should be found for George's wife to travel and spend the night in the hotel with him (for she had never been to London), this was agreed upon. The big day arrived, the deputy head's bright red car had been decorated with streamers and he drove to George's home to pick him up with his wife. Children lined the route, many parents turned out, in fact, most of the village appeared to be there as the car slowly made its way to the station amidst clapping, cheering and flag waving. After being interviewed the next morning George 'phoned the school to say he had gained third place and won a gold watch. Messages were sent to all the classes informing them. At our next assembly George and his wife came and he proudly showed his watch to the children. Both said they had enjoyed a wonderful time in London in a luxury hotel and that all the people they had met had been extremely kind. Needless to say George's fame quickly spread and several articles appeared in the local press about his success.

Other members of the school community are valuable resources, for example, secretary, mid-day supervisor, caretaker and cook. In fact the cook was used as an important part of a health, hygiene and safety project. Interaction with the wider community involved a host of parents who came in to talk about and illustrate their jobs and interests, for example, a musician, dentist, policeman, plumber, a Japanese mother demonstrating Origami, market gardener, graphic designer and miner, amongst others. The children went out into the community visiting the library, home for the disabled, old age pensioners' afternoon tea and the church, as well as conducting different surveys.

Coping with adversity

At the end of a summer term, a parent who was also a mid-day supervisor remarked, 'Mrs Tattum, you have had an awful year.' She was referring to the fact that in the class of children I had taught that year three families had lost a parent, two mothers and a father had died, and one of my nine year olds had suffered a serious road accident.

During the month of January, before the children returned to school after the Christmas holiday Ceri had been knocked down by a car, she ran across the road to speak to a friend and the wing mirror of the vehicle struck her head. She suffered severe brain damage and lay in a coma for three weeks. It was most distressing seeing her in this state. The specialist urged visitors to speak to her even though her eyes were closed and she couldn't move, in the hope that the stimulation would bring some response from her.

All the children were very upset, Ceri was a popular member of our class, she was a chatterbox, very lively and had a good sense of humour, frequently playing tricks on her friends. Several mothers were approached and as a result close friends were taken to visit Ceri on a rota basis after school. We held a discussion in class looking for ideas as to how we could help. Some of the boys volunteered that she used to tease them and call them names like handsome, hulk and mouse. Four of the girls talked about the Christmas concert and their dance routine with Ceri in the storm sequence to the Thunder and Lightning Polka, how Ceri was always complaining that teacher was showing them the wrong steps! We decided it would be a good idea to take the tape of the music when we next visited the hospital. Another idea came up about making a tape of all the children in the class individually saying hello and bearing a message reminiscing about some incident which had occurred over the term, for example spilling the paint on the floor, a TV programme, stories they had enjoyed, collecting blackberries on the school field, the nicknames of the boys and many more. When the recording had been made we took it to the hospital. By this time Ceri had opened her eyes but was still dangerously ill. The recorded messages were played several times and Ceri's mother excitedly remarked she saw a faint smile appear on Ceri's face. On repeating the recording we were all able to see how the reminiscing brought a more positive response from her. The tape was left with the nurse for her to use whenever she wished.

The four girls involved in the dance routine were taken on the next visit to hospital. They stood at the bedside and spoke to Ceri reminding her about the fun they'd had rehearsing the dance, then the music was played. The nurses became quite excited for Ceri's legs were moving beneath the sheets, the tune was clearly getting through to her. Our hopes were raised and the 'dancers' couldn't wait to get back to school next day to share their joy with the class. Ceri was allowed home during early summer but had to attend the hospital regularly for physiotherapy and speech therapy, as she found walking and talking most difficult. Ceri's mother came to class and said Ceri was impatient to come back to school so we arranged three half days a week to start with in case she became too tired. The long awaited time arrived and Ceri walked into class, a cheer went up and everyone clapped. 'She's here, she's here,' they all cried, 'Ceri's back!'.

In a number of ways the class also helped and supported fellow members who were coping with serious illness and bereavement in the family.

The integration of Julian by the whole class

The integration of children with special needs is probably more to do with giving them opportunities to interact with other children on an equal basis than it is to do with the curriculum. There is a need for the teacher to plan social interactive opportunities so that the child is accepted into the class and is assisted into acquiring appropriate social skills.

Julian was an eight year old boy whose parents came to live in the village and he was transferred to my class from a residential school for children with emotional and behavioural difficulties. Julian had many problems, he was constantly attention seeking and determined to interrupt lessons with irrelevances, singing 'Ho Ho the Wokey Cokey', barking like a dog, shouting 'Hello everyone' on his return from the toilet and always saying 'Why?' to everything he was told to do. He enjoyed the attention of having extra help with his work, I explained to him that this wasn't always possible as other children needed my help too. The children on his table helped him willingly with spellings, dictionary work and reading difficulties, as he was more capable of coping with Maths. The class was told that not only Julian needed their support in getting him to improve his behaviour but I needed it too (Julian had been sent to the Head to read a passage from his reading book), so discussion took place as to how this improvement could be brought about, for example ignoring his comments, baby talk and calling out, by telling him that he was disturbing them and if he wanted their cooperation and friendship he should show more consideration for others. Julian's mother regularly came to school to enquire about him and was pleased to help with his reading at home. He had been quite lonely when they first moved into the village but talked about several children in the class being kind to him. Friendships had always presented a problem to him because of his immaturity. He frequently got into mischief at weekends, there were incidences of him 'stealing' the milk float and driving it down the road, dropping stones into the letter box and knocking on doors.

Before our weekly visit to the public library across the road the class were reminded again about good behaviour and showing respect for others. This visit would be a new experience for Julian so we all kept our fingers crossed. The librarian spotted a new face in our class and spoke kindly to Julian asking him his name. Julian told him and said, 'What's yours?'. In spite of his loud whispering, the members of the public were most tolerant. One elderly gentleman who seemed to time his visit with our Tuesday appearances said he looked forward to seeing us again next week. On returning to class Julian was praised and it was decided he should be rewarded with five house points. Next day Mandy complained her roll of sweets was missing from her bag – several children mentioned stealing and suspicion hung over the class, we urged her to look in her drawer and bag again. On doing so it was discovered the sweets had fallen through the lining into the bottom of the bag. She apologised and said she was glad they had not been stolen, we all agreed. I said it was always better to tell the truth no matter how difficult it is or how embarrassing the circumstances may be. At this Julian put his hand up to own up to drawing a black line on William's shirt sleeve during a TV programme. 'It was only a little one', he said. William admitted he hadn't even noticed! All the class were invited to Andy's party, they wrote their thank you acceptance notes. Julian thoroughly enjoyed himself at the party. He won a game and said he would be having a party on his birthday too. Julian now collected the attendance register each day and took it to the office, the secretaries always praised his politeness. One Tuesday afternoon the wet weather made us decide that it would be foolish to walk to the library and that the librarian should be informed of our decision. Julian was chosen to ask the Head if he could use the phone and make apologies on our behalf. He conveyed the message in a capable manner and the librarian thanked Julian for letting him know. As weeks went by the children continued to support Julian and encouraged him in every possible way so that he became more accepted and socialised into the ways of doing things in the class.

Julian continued to behave in this positive manner for the rest of his time in the village school. During holidays he would call at the house and say hello, admire the garden and on one occasion to show me his new bicycle. At the end of the fourth year Julian transferred to a secondary school with a strong remedial department where his parents felt that it would be more beneficial for him to study. After two years of attending there, his father's work meant that the family had to move to another area. Julian called at the house to say goodbye but reminded me that in the future he would be visiting the village again to call on his friends.

Respecting the rights of others

Female teachers predominate in primary schools therefore there is a danger the social education of boys may not be adequately catered for. Football is a consuming interest with boys in the upper junior classes and female teachers should make a conscious effort to familiarise themselves with the sport, the major clubs, the rules of the game, the results and so on. They must enter the boys' world. Every Monday morning I talked about the weekend matches – they all knew that I was a fervent Liverpool supporter. The other side of the coin is that at playtime the boys' interests dominated the playground much to the distress of the girls. This problem was frequently discussed and talked through as to how they could respect the rights of each other and the younger children too. Every school should have a discussion about how to equalise opportunities at playtime. First of all there should be a zoned area for the boys to play their ball games and a practice area for netball. The different age ranges should be catered for as far as possible. The younger children need a place to sit. Depending on the type of playground and surrounding area it could be possible with the help of parents to plant shrubs to attract birds and butterflies, and containers with spring flowering bulbs and summer bedding plants. Children could be enlisted to help stencil a hopscotch area, giant chess boards, snakes and ladders and concentric circles for other popular games – students from the local comprehensive school could supervise and help with this work. Ugly walls can be transformed with murals, for example on one wall of the yard colourful hot air balloons had been painted much to the delight of the children, they were frequently studied and used for a teaching aid as well. A dull wall could also be brightened up by using an alphabet or number frieze in the infant section of the yard. At every stage children should always be invited to offer ideas and plans for improvement of their play area.

The media can be used as a positive resource for discussion of items that appear in the news or newspapers or current affairs programmes. Children can be asked to bring in items from the media which they can develop around the theme of tolerance and equality.

Individual children's interests can be used to raise their self-esteem and status in the eyes of the rest of the class. Different children talked about and demonstrated things like fishing, judo, scuba diving, horse riding, dolls in national costume and two children ably performed a magic show.

In conclusion

The title of the book *Social Education and Personal Development* was deliberately chosen because we wished to emphasise the fact that social education, however delivered, aims to change the child in fundamental ways. In essence, we each hold dearly to certain values, beliefs and attitudes and in our teaching we demonstrate them by what we praise and what we criticise; by the topics we choose and the direction in which they are developed; by the way we organise our classes, discipline children, and the quality of the relationships we invite (or otherwise). Therefore, it is vitally important that we have an understanding of the social processes operating in a school and how they influence a child's personal development.

Children are not born social beings but learn from the social experiences adults present them with, and schools are a very important part of this socialisation process. Above all else school provides a unique social world for children. From the time they enter reception class and subsequent age-classes the quality of relationships is paramount. Schools can make a difference, not only to the academic performance of children, but to their social development as wholesome and integrated members of the community. But the conditions for social and personal development have to be created and how we organise pupil's social experiences is one of the challenges facing primary schools in the next decade.

References

ACE (1990) *Governors and Bullying*. Bulletin 34, ACE, London.

Ahmad, Y. and Smith, P. K. (1990) 'Bully/victim problems among school-children'. Poster paper presented at conference of the Developmental Section of the BPS, Guildford.

Ahmad, Y., Whitney, B. and Smith, P. K. (1991) 'A survey service for schools on bully/victim problems'. In Smith and Thompson (eds.) (1991).

Allport, G. W. (1961) *Pattern and Growth in Personality*. Holt, Rinehart & Winston, New York.

AMMA (1984) 'The reception class today', Report, 7 (i), pp. 6–9.

AMMA (1987) *Starting School: An AMMA Digest*. AMMA, London.

Ashton, P. M., Kneen, P., Davies, F. R. and Holley, B. J. (1974) *The Aims of Primary Education*. Macmillan, London.

Austin, R. (1986) 'The dividing line', *Junior Education*, 10, (11), November.

Baldwin, J. and Wells, H. (1979–84) *Active Tutorial Work*. Blackwell, Oxford.

Barker Lunn, J. C. (1970) *Streaming in the Primary School*. NFER, Windsor.

Baumrind, D. (1971) 'Current patterns of paternal authority', *Developmental Psychology Monographs*, 4 (1, Part 2).

Becker, H. (1952) 'Social class variations in the teacher–pupil relationship', *Journal of Educational Sociology*, 25, (4), pp. 451–65.

Beez, W. V. (1968) 'Influence of biased psychological reports on teacher behaviour and pupil performance'. Proceedings of the 76th Annual Convention of the American Psychological Association, No 3, pp. 605–6.

Bennett, S. N. (1985) 'Interaction and achievement in classroom groups'. In S. N. Bennett and C. Desfarges *Recent Advances in Classroom Research*, *British Journal of Educational Psychology*. Monograph series, No.2, Scottish Academic Press, pp. 105–19.

Berger, P. L. and Berger, B. (1976 Revised edn.) *Sociology: A Biographical Approach*. Penguin, Harmondsworth.

Berger, P. L. and Luckmann, T. (1967) *The Social Construction of Reality*. Penguin, Harmondsworth.

Berndt, T. J. (1982) 'The features and effects of friendship in early adolescence', *Childhood Development*, 53, pp. 1447–60.

Bernstein, B. (1970a) 'Elaborated and restricted codes: their social origins and some consequences'. In K. Danziger (ed.) *Readings in Child Socialisation*. Pergamon, Oxford.

Bernstein, B. (1970b) 'A critique of the concept of compensatory education'. In D. Rubenstein and C. Stoneman (eds.) *Education for Democracy*, Penguin, Harmondsworth.

Bernstein, B. (1971) *Class, Codes and Control, Vol. 1*. Routledge & Kegan Paul, London.

Besag, V. (1989) *Bullies and Victims in Schools*. OU Press, Milton Keynes.

Blatchford, P. (1989) *Playtime in the Primary School. Problems and Improvements*. NFER-Nelson, Windsor.

Blatchford, P., Creeser, R. and Mooney, A. (1990) 'Playground games and playtime; the children's view'. *Educational Research*, 32, (2), pp. 163–74.

Bledsoe, J. C. (1967) 'Bledsoe Self-concept Scale'. In W. W. Purkey 'The search for self', *Childhood Education*, 43.

Bossert, S. (1987) 'Classroom task organisation and children's friendships'. In A. Pollard (ed.) *Children and their Primary Schools*, Falmer Press, London.

Brophy, J. and Good, T. (1970) 'Teachers' communication of differential expectations for children's classroom performance: some behavioural data', *Journal of Educational Psychology*, 61, pp. 365–74.

Brophy, J. and Good, T. (1974) 'Changing teacher and student behaviour: an empirical investigation', *Journal of Educational Psychology*, 66, 3.

Bukowski, W. M. and Hoza, B. (1989) 'Popularity and friendship; issues in theory, measurement and outcome'. In T. J. Berndt and G. W. Ladd (eds.) *Peer Relationships in Child Development*, Wiley, New York.

Burns, R. B. (1982) *Self-Concept Development and Education*. Holt, Rinehart & Winston, London.

Burns, R. B. (1986) *Child Development. A Text for the Caring Professions*. Croom Helm, London.

Button, L. (1981) *Group Tutoring for the Form Teacher*. Hodder & Stoughton, London.

Child, I. L. (1943) *Italian or American*. Yale University Press, Boston.

Cohen, L. and Cohen, A. (1970) 'Attributes of success in primary school – some conflicting beliefs of teachers and parents', *Durham Research Review*, 24, pp. 449–54.

Cooley, C. H. (1902) *Human Nature and the Social Order*. Charles Scribner, New York.

Cowie, H. (1987) 'Perceptions of group work by pupils and teachers', *Educational and Child Psychology*, 4, (3), pp. 19–28.

Cranfield, J. and Wells, H. (1976) *100 Ways to Enhance Self-concept in the Classroom*. Prentice-Hall, New Jersey.

Crano, W. D. and Mellon, D. M. (1978) 'Casual influence of teacher expectations on children's academic performance: a cross-lagged panel analysis', *Journal of Educational Psychology*, 70, pp. 39–49.

CRE (1988) *Learning in Terror! A survey of racial harassment in schools and colleges*. Commission for Racial Equality, London.

Davie, R., Butler, N. and Goldstein, H. (1972) *From Birth to Seven*. Longman, London.

Davies, B. (1982) *Life in the Classroom and Playground. The Accounts of Primary School Children*. Routledge & Kegan Paul, London.

Davies, G. (1986) *A First Year Tutorial Handbook*. Blackwell, Oxford.

Davis, K. (1947) 'Final Notes on a Case of Extreme Isolation', *American Journal of Sociology*, 52, pp. 432–7.

Duke, D. L. (1978) 'Looking at the school as a rule-governed organisation', *Journal of Research and Development in Education*, 11, (4), pp. 116–26.

Elkin, F. (1960) *The Child and Society*. Random House, New York.

Elliott, M. (ed.) (1991) *Bullying: A Practical Guide to Coping for Schools*. Longman, Harlow.

Elton Report (1989) *Discipline in Schools*. HMSO, London.

Frude, N. (1984) 'Framework for analysis'. In N. Frude and H. Gault *Disruptive Behaviour in Schools*, Wiley, Chichester.

Galton, M., Simon, B. and Croll, P. (1980) *Inside the Primary Classroom*. Routledge & Kegan Paul, London.

Galton, M. and Willcock, J. (1983) *Moving from the Primary Classroom*. Routledge & Kegan Paul, London.

Galton, M., Patrick, H., Appleyard, R., Hargreaves, L. and Bernbaum, G. (1987) 'Curriculum provisions in small schools: the PRISMS project', Final Report, University of Leicester (mimeo).

Galton, M. (1990) 'Grouping and groupwork'. In C. Rogers and P. Kutnick *The Social Psychology of the Primary School*. Routledge, London.

Garwood, S. G. and McDavid, J. W. (1975) 'Ethnic factors in stereotypes of given names', *Resources in Education*, Georgia State University.

Garwood, S. G. (1976) 'First name stereotypes as a factor in self-concept and school achievement', *Journal of Educational Psychology*, 68, (4).

Geer, B. (1968) 'Teaching'. In D. S. Sills (ed.) *International Encyclopedia of the Social Sciences*, Free Press, New York.

Glock, M. D. (1972) 'Is there a Pygmalion in the classroom', *The Reading Teacher*, 25, pp. 405–8.

Goffman, E. (1968) *Asylums*. Penguin, Harmondsworth.

Goffman, E. (1969) *The Presentation of Self in Everyday Life*. Penguin, Harmondsworth.

Good, T. L. and Brophy, J. E. (1984) *Looking in Classrooms*, 2nd edition. Harper & Row, New York.

Halperin, M. S. (1976) 'First grade teachers' goals and children's developing perceptions of schools', *Journal of Educational Psychology*, 68, pp. 636–48.

Hamblin, D. H. (1978) *The Teacher and Pastoral Care*. Blackwell, Oxford.

Harari, H. and McDavid, J. W. (1973) 'Name stereotypes and teacher expectations' *Journal of Educational Psychology*, 65, (2).

Hargreaves, D. H. (1967) *Social Relations in a Secondary School*. Routledge & Kegan Paul, London.

Hargreaves, D. H., Hester, S. K. and Mellor, F. J. (1975) *Deviance in Classrooms*. Routledge & Kegan Paul, London.

Hartup, W. W. (1983) 'Peer relationships'. In P. H. Mussen (ed.) *Handbook of Child Psychology*, Vol. 4, Wiley, New York.

Heiss, J. (1981) *The Social Psychology of Interaction*. Prentice-Hall, New Jersey.

Herbert, G. (1988) 'A whole-curriculum approach to bullying'. In D. Tattum and D. Lane (1988).

Hewitt, J. P. (1976) *Self and Society*. Allyn & Bacon, Boston.

HMI (1987) *Education Observed 5. Good Behaviour and Discipline in Schools*. HMSO, London.

HMI (1988) *Secondary Schools. An appraisal by HMI*. HMSO, London.

HMI (1989) *Education Observed 13. Attendance at School*. HMSO, London.

Hollingsworth, E. J., Lufler, H. S. and Clune, W. H. (1984) *School Discipline: Order and Autonomy*. Praeger, New York.

Holt, J. (1969) *How Children Fail*. Penguin, Harmondsworth.

Jackson, P. W. (1968) *Life in Classrooms*. Holt, Rinehart & Winston, New York.

Johnson, D. W. and Johnson, R. T. (1987) *Learning Together and Alone* (2nd edition). Prentice-Hall, New Jersey.

Kando, T. M. (1977) *Social Interaction*. C. V. Mosby Co., St. Louis.

Kelly, E. and Cohn, T. (1988) *Racism in Schools – New Research Evidence*. Trentham Books, Stoke-on-Trent.

Kerry, T. and Sands, M. (1982) *Handling Classroom Groups*. University of Nottingham, School of Education (mimeo).

Knox, P. (1988) *Troubled Children. A Fresh Look at School Phobia*. Pat Knox, Holyhead, North Wales.

Kutnick, P. (1983) *Relating to Learning*. Allen & Unwin, London.

Kutnick, P. (1988) *Relationships in the Primary School Classroom*. Paul Chapman, London.

Labov, W. (1969) 'Some sources of reading problems for negro speakers of nonstandard English'. In J. C. Baratz and R. Shuy (eds.) *Teaching Black Children to Read*, Center for Applied Linguistics, Washington, D.C.

Lacey, C. (1970) *Hightown Grammar*. Manchester University Press, Manchester.

Laing, A. F. and Chazan, M. (1986) 'The management of aggressive behaviour in young children'. In D. P. Tattum (ed.) (1986).

Lang, P. (1988a) *Thinking About . . . Personal and Social Education in the Primary School*. Blackwell, Oxford.

Lang, P. (1988b) 'Primary and middle school teachers' attitudes to pastoral provision and personal and social education'. In P. Lang (ed.) *Thinking About . . . Personal and Social Education in the Primary School*, Blackwell, Oxford.

Langer, J. (1969) *Theories of Development*. Holt, Rinehart & Winston, New York.

Lawrence, J., Steed, D. and Young, P. (1986) 'The management of disruptive behaviour in Western Europe'. In D. P. Tattum (1986).

Leach, P. (1989) *Smacking – a Short-cut to Nowhere*. EPOCH, London.

Lemert, E. M. (1951) *Social Pathology*. McGraw-Hill, New York.

Lindesmith, A. R., Strauss, A. L. and Denzin, N. K. (1977) *Social Psychology*. Holt, Rinehart & Winston, New York.

Lufler, H. S., Jr. (1979) 'Debating the untested assumptions. The need to understand school discipline'. *Education and Urban Society*, 11, (4), pp. 450–64.

MacDonald, I., Bhavnani, R., Kahn, L. and John, G. (1989) *Murder in the Playground. The Report of the MacDonald Inquiry into Racism and Racist Violence in Manchester Schools*. Longsight Press, London.

Marsh, H. W. and Shavelson, R. (1985) 'Self-concept: its multifaceted, hierarchical structure', *Educational Psychologist*, 20, pp. 107–23.

Maxwell, W. (1990) 'The nature of friendship in the primary school'. In C. Rogers and P. Kutnick (1990).

McGuire, K. D. and Weisz, J. R. (1982) 'Social cognition and behaviour correlates of pre-adolescent chumship', *Child Development*, 53, pp. 1478–84.

Mead, G. H. (1956) In A. Strauss (ed.) *On Social Psychology: Selected Papers*. University of Chicago Press, Chicago.

Measor, L. and Woods, P. (1984) *Changing Schools: Pupil Perspectives on Transfer to a Comprehensive*. OU Press, Milton Keynes.

Meighan, R. (1978) 'A pupil's eye view of teaching performance', *Education Review*, 29, (2), pp. 123–35.

Meighan, R. (1986) *A Sociology of Education* (2nd edition). Holt, Rinehart & Winston, New York.

Mellor, A. (1990) 'Bullying in Scottish secondary schools', *Spotlights*, No. 23, Scottish Council for Research in Education.

Meltzer, B. N., Petras, J. W. and Reynolds, J. (1975) *Symbolic Interactionism: Genesis Varieties and Criticism*. Routledge & Kegan Paul, London.

Mooij, T. (1991) Personal communication, September, 1991.

Mortimore, P., Sammons, P., Stoll, L., Lewis, D. and Ecob, R. (1987) *The Junior School Project*. ILEA (Research and Statistics Branch) (mimeo).

Nash, R. (1974) 'Pupil expectations of their teacher'. In M. Stubbs and S. Delamont (eds.) *Explorations in Classroom Observation*, Wiley, Chichester.

National Association of Head Teachers (1984) *Council Memorandum on Discipline in Schools*. NAHT, Haywoods Heath.

National Curriculum Council (Oct. 1989) 'The National Curriculum and whole curriculum planning: preliminary guidance', Circular No. 6, NCC, York.

National Curriculum Council (1990) *Education for Citizenship*. NCC, York.

Newson, J. (1974) 'Towards a theory of infant understanding', *Bulletin of the British Psychological Society*, 27, pp. 251 7.

Newson, J. and Newson, E. (1976) *Seven Years Old in the Home Environment*. Allen & Unwin, London. (Published in paperback by Penguin, 1978.)

Newson, J., Newson, E. and Barnes, P. (1977) *Perspectives on School at Seven Years Old*. Allen & Unwin, London.

Newson, J. and Newson, E. (1989) *The Extent of Parental Physical Punishment in the UK*. APPROACH, London.

Olweus, D. (1978) *Aggression in the Schools: Bullies and Whipping Boys*. Wiley, Washington, D.C.

Olweus, D. (1984) 'Aggressors and their victims: bullying at school'. In N. Frude and H. Gault (eds.) *Disruptive Behaviour in Schools*, Wiley, Chichester.

Olweus, D. (1988) 'Bully/victim problems among school children: basic facts and effects of a School Based Intervention Program'. In K. Rubin and D. Pepler (eds.) *The Development and Treatment of Childhood Aggression*, Erlbaum, New Jersey.

O'Moore, A. M. (1988) *Bullying in Schools*. (Council of Europe Report, DECSEGT (88) 5-E). Council for Cultural Cooperation, Strasbourg.

O'Moore, A. M. and Hillery, B. (1991) 'What do teachers need to know?'. In M. Elliot (ed.) *Bullying: A Practical Guide to Coping for Schools*, Longman, Harlow.

Opie, I. and Opie, P. (1959) *The Lore and Language of Schoolchildren*. Oxford University Press, London.

Opie, I. and Opie, P. (1969) *Children's Games in Street and Playground*. Oxford University Press, London.

OPTIS (1986) *Lunchtime Supervision* (2nd edition). Oxfordshire Programme for Training, Oxford.

Open University, E282, Units 5 to 8 (1972) *The Social Organisation of Teaching and Learning*. Open University Press, Milton Keynes.

Open University, E200, Unit 3 (1981) *Learning in the Family*. Open University Press, Milton Keynes.

Open University, D207, Block 1 (1980) *Socialisation: conformity and opposition*. Open University Press, Milton Keynes.

Palardy, J. M. (1969) 'What teachers believe – what children achieve', *Elementary School Journal*, 69.

Partington, J. T. and Grant, C. (1984) 'Imaginery playmates and other useful fantasies'. In P. K. Smith (ed.) *Play in Animals and Humans*. Blackwell, Oxford.

Peters, R. S. (1966) *Ethics and Education*. Allen & Unwin, London.

Piaget, J. (1926) *Language and Thought of the Child*. Basic Books, New York.

Piaget, J. (1932) *The Moral Judgement of the Child*. Penguin, Harmondsworth.

Piaget, J. (1951) *Play, Dreams and Imitation in Childhood*. Routledge & Kegan Paul, London.

Piaget, J. (1952) *The Child's Concept of Number*. Routledge & Kegan Paul, London.

Pidgeon, D. A. (1970) *Expectations and Pupil Performance*. NFER, Slough.

Plowden Report (1967) *Children and their Primary Schools*, Vol. 1. HMSO, London.

Pollard, A. (1985) *The Social World of the Primary School*. Holt, Rinehart & Winston, London.

Pollard, A. (1986) 'An ethnographic analysis of classroom conflict'. In D. P. Tattum (ed.) (1986).

Pring, R. (1988) 'Personal and social education in the primary school'. In P. Lang (ed.) (1988).

Quine, W. G. (1974) 'Polarized cultures in comprehensive schools', *Research in Education*, 12, pp. 41–50.

Reid, K. (1981) 'Alienation and persistent school absenteeism', *Research in Education*, 26, pp. 31–40.

Reid, K. (1985) *Truancy and School Absenteeism*. Hodder & Stoughton, London.

Reid, K. (1988) 'Bullying and persistent school absenteeism'. In D. P. Tattum and D. A. Lane (1988).

Reid, K. (1989) *Helping Troubled Pupils in Secondary Schools, Vol. 2.* Blackwell, Oxford.

Reynolds, D., Jones, D. and St. Leger, S. (1976) 'Schools do make a difference', *New Society*, 37, (721), pp. 223–5.

Rigby, K. and Slee, P. T. (1990) 'Victims and bullies in school communities', *Journal of the Australian Society of Victimology*, 1, (2), pp. 23–8.

Rist, R. G. (1970) 'Student social class and teacher expectation: the self-fulfilling prophecy', *Harvard Educational Review*, 40, pp. 411–15.

Rogers, C. (1982) *The Social Psychology of Schooling*. Routledge & Kegan Paul, London.

Rogers, C. and Kutnick, P. (1990) *The Social Psychology of the Primary School*. Routledge, London.

Roland, E. (1988) 'Bullying: the Scandinavian research tradition'. In D. P. Tattum and D. A. Lane (1988).

Roland, E. and Munthe, E. (1989) *Bullying. An International Perspective*. David Fulton, London.

Roland, E. (1991) Personal communication, September, 1991.

Rosenberg, M. (1979) *Conceiving the Self*. Basic Books, New York.

Rosenthal, R. and Jacobson, L. (1968) *Pygmalion in the Classroom*. Holt, Rinehart & Winston, New York.

Ross, C. and Ryan, A. (1990) *Can I stay in today Miss? Improving the School Playground*. Trentham Books, Stoke-on-Trent.

Rubin, Z. (1980) *Children's Friendships*. Fontana, London.

Rutter, M., Maughan, B., Mortimore, P., Ouston, J. and Smith, A. (1979) *Fifteen Thousand Hours: Secondary Schools and Their Effects on Children*. Open Books, London.

Schaefer, E. S. (1959) 'A circumflex model of maternal behaviour', *Journal of Abnormal and Social Psychology*, 59, (232).

Schaffer, H. R. (1971) *The Growth of Sociability*. Penguin, Harmondsworth.

Schaffer, R. (1988) 'Face-to-face interactions'. In W. Woodhead and A. McGrath (eds.) *Family, School and Society*, Hodder & Stoughton, London.

Schunk, D. H. (1990) 'Self-concept and school achievement'. In C. Rogers and P. Kutnick.

Shibutani, T. (1955) 'Reference groups in perspective', *American Journal of Sociology*, LX, pp. 562–9.

Shipman, M. D. (1972) *Childhood. A Sociological Perspective*. NFER, Slough.

Slavin, R. E. (1983) *Cooperative Learning*. Longman, New York.

Slavin, R. E. (1985) 'Cooperative learning: applying contact theory in desegregated schools', *Journal of Social Issues*, 41, pp. 45–62.

Slavin, R. E. (1986) *Using Student Team Learning* (3rd edition), Centre for Research in Elementary and Middle Schools, Johns Hopkins University Press, Baltimore.

186

Slavin, R. E. (1990) 'Cooperative learning'. In C. Rogers and P. Kutnick (1990).

Sluckin, A. (1981) *Growing up in the Playground: The Social Development of Children*. Routledge & Kegan Paul, London.

Sluckin, A. (1987) 'The culture of the primary school playground'. In A. Pollard (ed.) *Children and their Primary Schools*. Falmer Press, London.

Smilansky, T. (1968) *The Effects of Sociodramatic Play on Disadvantaged Preschool Children*. Wiley, New York.

Smith, P. K. (1990) 'The role of play in the nursery and primary school'. In C. Rogers and P. Kutnick (1990).

Smith, P. K. and Cowie, H. (1991) *Understanding Children's Development* (2nd edition). Blackwell, Oxford.

Smith, P. K. and Thompson, P. (eds.) (1991) *Practical Approaches to Bullying*. David Fulton, London.

Stephenson, P. and Smith, D. (1988) 'Bullying in the junior school'. In D. P. Tattum and D. A. Lane (1988).

Stoate, P. and Thacker, J. (1988) 'Application of developmental group work principles to personal and social education in primary and middle schools'. In P. Lang (1988).

Sullivan, H. S. (1953) *The Interpersonal Theory of Psychiatry*. Norton, New York.

Tattum, D. P. (1982) *Disruptive Pupils in Schools and Units*. Wiley, Chichester.

Tattum, D. P. (ed.) (1986) *Disruptive Pupil Management*. David Fulton, London.

Tattum, D. P. (1988) 'Social education is interaction'. In P. Lang (1988).

Tattum, D. P. and Lane, D. A. (eds.) (1988) *Bullying in Schools*. Trentham Books, Stoke-on-Trent.

Tattum, D. P. (1989a) 'Alternative approaches to disruptive behaviour'. In N. Jones (ed.) *School Management and Pupil Behaviour*. Falmer Press, London.

Tattum, D. P. (1989b) 'Violent, aggressive and disruptive behaviour'. In N. Jones (ed.) *Special Educational Needs Review*, Vol. I. Falmer Press, London.

Tattum, D. P. (1989c) 'Disruptive behaviour: a whole-school approach'. In K. Reid (1989).

Tattum, D. P. (1989d) 'Bullying – a problem crying out for attention', *Pastoral Care in Education*, 7, (2), pp. 21–5.

Tattum, D. P. (1989e) 'Reign of terror: school bullies and their victims', *Childright*, 56, pp. 18–19.

Tattum, D. P. and Herbert, G. (1990) *Bullying: A Positive Response. Advice for Parents, Governors and Staff in Schools*. Cardiff Institute of Higher Education, Cardiff.

Tattum, D. P. and Herbert, G. (1992) *Bullying: A Whole-School Response*, Video Films and Resource Pack. Drake Educational Associates, Cardiff.

Tattum, D. P. and Tattum, E. (1992) 'Bullying: A whole-school response'. In N. Jones (ed.) *School Discipline and Whole School Management*, Cassells, London.

187

Tizard, B., Blatchford, P., Burke, J., Farquhar, C. and Plewis, I. (1988) *Young Children at School in the Inner City*. Erlbaum, London.
Topping, K. (1986) 'Consultative enhancement of school-based action'. In D. P. Tattum (1986).
Tyerman, M. J. (1968) *Truancy*. University of London Press, London.
Vygotsky, L. S. (1962) *Thought and Language*. MIT Press, Cambridge, Mass.
Watkins, C. and Wagner, P. (1987) *School Discipline: A Whole-School Approach*. Blackwell, Oxford.
Watson, J. B. (1924) *Behaviourism*. University of Chicago Press, Chicago.
Watson, M. W. (1981) 'The development of social roles: a sequence of social-cognitive development', *New Directions for Child Development*, 12, pp. 33–41.
Webster, M. and Sobieszek, B. (1974) *Sources of Self Evaluation*. Wiley, New York.
Weston, P., Taylor, P. H. and Hurman, A. (1978) 'Client's expectations of secondary schooling', *Educational Review*, 30, (2), pp. 159–66.
Wicks, M. (August, 1990) 'The battle for the family, *Marxism Today*, pp. 28–33.
Wilson, J. (1989) 'Non-attenders'. In K. Reid (1989).
Withey, D. A. (1979) 'Rewards in school: some sociological perspectives', *Doddum and Newcastle Review*, 9, pp. 22–6.
Woods, P. (1978) *The Divided School*. Routledge & Kegan Paul, London.
Woods, P. (1983) *Sociology and the School. An Interactionist Viewpoint*. Routledge & Kegan Paul, London.
Wright, D. S. (1962) 'A comparative study of the adolescent's concept of his parents and teachers', *Educational Review*, 14, (3), pp. 226–32.
Wrong, D. (1961) 'The over-socialized conception of man in modern society', *American Sociological Review*, 26, pp. 184–93.
Yates, C. and Smith, P. K. (1989) 'Bullying in two English comprehensive schools'. In E. Roland and E. Munthe.
Yeomans, A. (1983) 'Collaborative group work in primary schools, Britain and USA', *Durham and Newcastle Research Review*, X, (51), pp. 99–105.
Youngman, M. B. and Lunzer, E. (1977) *Adjustment to Secondary School*. University of Nottingham, School of Education.
Ziegler, S. and Rosenstein-Manner, M. (1991) *Bullying at School: Toronto in an International Context* (No. 196R), Research Services, Toronto Board of Education.
Zimmerman, I. L. and Allebrand, G. N. (1968) 'Personality characteristics and attitudes toward achievement of good and poor readers', *Journal of Educational Psychology*, 59, pp. 28–30.

Author Index

Subject Index